C H O I

Cheryl Thomas Peters, D.T.R.

Meals you can make in 30 minutes or less

Review and Herald® Publishing Association
Hagerstown, MD 21740

ACKNOWLEDGEMENTS

Susan Harvey ♦ *Editor*

Meyer Design ♦ *Cookbook Designer*

Robin Meyer ♦ *Art Director*

Paul Poplis ♦ *Photographer*

Carmen Himes ♦ *Food Stylist*

Kathy Walsh ♦ *Assistant Food Stylist*

The author assumes full responsibility for the accuracy of all facts and quotations as cited in this book.

Copyright © 1994
Review and Herald® Publishing Association
PRINTED IN U.S.A.
98 97   10 9 8 7 6 5

R&H Cataloging Service

Peters, Cheryl Thomas, 1962-

    Choices: quick and healthy cooking.

    1. Vegetarian cookery.   I. Title.

       641.5636

An ASI Student Project

ISBN 0-8280-0847-7

Dedication

To my son, Kent, who exclaims after almost every meal, "Thank you, Mamma, that was the best food I ever had!" With encouragement like that as I wrote this book, how could I not succeed!

Acknowledgments

My heart-felt thanks to all the family and friends who contributed their recipes, ideas, and inspiration. Also, a special thanks to those who attended my seminars and encouraged me to write this book.

My gratitude to all those who contributed their individual talents to make this book a success, including Susan Harvey, the editor; Paul Poplis, the food photographer; Carmen Himes and Kathy Walsh, the food stylists; and Robin Meyer, the book designer. I'd also like to thank Jay Highman, of Worthington Foods, who provided sample food products for me to experiment with, as well as guidance in creative areas, including design and photography; and Greg Antill, Test Kitchen Supervisor at Worthington Foods, for nutritional analysis data.

CONTENTS

A New Way of Shopping, Cooking, and Eating

This book began as the result of a personal challenge. It was a long time in coming. From my earliest years, my mother taught me how to prepare balanced meatless meals. As a young wife and mother, I combined that knowledge with my education in dietetics, learning how to decrease the fat in my repertoire of favorite recipes. But cooking healthfully was time-consuming! My time became even more limited as I took on the multiple roles of motherhood, minister's wife, author, and seminar speaker. I was faced with the increasingly difficult daily challenge of feeding my family nutritionally balanced and varied meatless meals that could be prepared in as short a time as possible.

Others faced the same problem. As I lectured in my Heart-Healthy Vegetarian seminars, the most frequently asked question was, "How do you find the time to cook like this?" Both for my own family and for those who attended my seminars, I set out to meet this challenge.

First, I set myself some guidelines: (1) to develop a plan for shopping, cooking, and eating that would fit into an overall healthy lifestyle; (2) to spend as little money on ingredients as possible without sacrificing quality; (3) to spend as little time in the kitchen and use as few utensils and pots and pans as possible, (4) to simplify the techniques for cooking foods low in cholesterol, fat, and sodium; (5) to adapt my favorite recipes (and those from family and friends) to make them healthier and easier to prepare without sacrificing taste; (6) to create new mouthwatering, nutritious, meatless meals in as

short a time as possible; and (7) to prepare eye-appealing foods that look as delicious as they taste.

What evolved from those rules is more than a cookbook. It is a new way of shopping, cooking, and eating. The *Choices* Eating-Right Plan uses only fine-quality ingredients, impeccably fresh, and turns them into delicious, plant-based meals with a minimum of fuss, concern, and time. Saving money is another bonus. With this plan, you'll buy fewer expensive prepared foods. The majority of your food budget will be spent in the fresh produce department of your supermarket, and to restock your staples such as grains, nuts, and legumes.

This cookbook details the plan, and provides a large selection of recipes for healthy breakfasts, lunches, and dinners. There are menu tips throughout, to help you combine foods with each main dish to create a nutritionally balanced meal.

Flexibility is provided by suggestions on varying the recipes to suit your taste, your dietary preferences, the size of your family, and the time you have available. In most cases, options are included for both the lacto-ovo and the vegan vegetarian. The plan works for a family of two or for a dinner party of 20.

Most of the main-dish recipes can be prepared in 30 minutes or less. Preparation and cooking times are shown with each recipe. (The two figures overlap and shouldn't be added together. For example, you may be sautéing some of the ingredients while chopping and preparing others.)

There are a few exceptions to the 30-minute limit. For instance, the time shown does not include cooking time for dried beans. The recipe will call for already cooked or canned beans. Choose which type you prefer, based on your preference and time limitations. Tips for preparing dried legumes are found on page 12.

Rice is another exception to the 30-minute rule. Preparation time given is based on using a rice cooker— one of my favorite kitchen helpers. Depending on the amount, whole-grain long grain rice cooks in roughly 35 minutes in a rice cooker, or in about 45-50 minutes on the stove. Some recipes will suggest that you use precooked or left-over rice to save time.

Getting organized and planning ahead are important elements in shortening last-minute preparation time. Some foods can be made ahead and kept in the freezer, such as piecrusts and homemade breads. Other made-ahead foods keep well in the refrigerator, such as precooked rice and beans, and the dairy and egg substitutes. These planned-ahead foods add great flexibility to the *Choices* plan.

The *Choices* Eating-Right Plan also involves keeping a well-stocked pantry, refrigerator, and freezer.

We're more likely to eat healthier if we have nutrient-high foods in the house. When cooking with less salt and fat, we must rely more on the good flavor of the natural food, and on high-quality herbs for seasoning. Select food of excellent quality, and store it carefully to preserve every bit of its freshness and flavor.

Of course, you and I know that eating right is not the only way to increase your chances of living a long, happy, healthy life. If you really want to look and feel your best, you need to do other things as well, such as get some exercise every day–preferably outdoors–drink lots of water, get adequate sleep, and reduce the stress and worry in your life. Be sure to read the section on The *Choices* Lifestyle Plan for suggestions on how to improve all areas of your life.

You may be surprised at how easily your family adapts to a healthier lifestyle. For instance, serving meatless meals is no longer considered an eccentric or unpopular thing to do, thanks to widening alarm about cholesterol and high-fat diets. Vegetarianism has evolved into a cuisine in its own right, no longer defined by what it lacks, but by the pleasures and benefits of eating simply prepared seasonal foods.

The Lifestyle Plan

Research done at the National Institutes of Health shows that two thirds of all deaths—including those caused by coronary heart diseases, strokes, atherosclerosis, diabetes, and some types of cancer—are related to our lifestyle choices, including what we eat. The top ten causes of death in the United States are associated with too much fat, calories, cholesterol, sugar, salt, alcohol, and tobacco; and too little fiber-rich foods.

Science doesn't have all the answers yet, but one thing is certain—right lifestyle choices can promote health and reduce the risk of disease dramatically. The ideas and recipes in this book are part of a lifestyle plan for optimum health and happiness. This *Choices* plan is the key to a happier, healthier you. Follow these eight principles, and you'll not only feel better and look better, you'll be better. **Here's the *Choices* list:**

1. Eat a wholesome plant-based diet.
2. Exercise daily.
3. Avoid drugs.
4. Drink eight glasses of water per day.
5. Spend some time—but not too much—in the sunlight when ever possible.
6. Enjoy fresh air every day.
7. Get adequate rest.
8. Put your trust in divine power.

Research has confirmed that this plan works. Much of the data for this research came from the largest government-sponsored scientific study ever done on vegetarians—known as the Adventist Health Study. Seventh-day Adventists abstain from using tobacco and alcohol, and about half are vegetarians. As a group, their lifestyle is useful to study in comparison with the average American lifestyle.

Research shows that "members of the Seventh-day Adventist Church are often acknowledged as the 'healthiest people in America.' In a nation with increasing cases of heart disease, obesity, osteoporosis, cancer, and other diet-related maladies, this group's adherents have managed to beat the odds. Study after study has found that members not only live longer, but experience fewer of the debilitating diseases that affect most Americans." "Diet for a Longer Life," *Saturday Evening Post*, January/February 1992.

Consider the following statistics from the above article:

Men from the above study group "have a life expectancy of 8.9 years longer than the average, while females have one that is 7.5 years longer."

Even though vegetarians, the study group had "a reduced risk of osteoporosis compared to meat eaters in the general population."

Study group participants "experience a lower incidence of breast, prostate, pancreatic, bladder, and ovarian cancers than the general population."

Those "who use no meat, milk, or eggs—total vegetarians—have an expected coronary

The Eating-Right Plan

heart disease mortality rate only 12 percent of that of the general population."

This study indicates that prevention of disease by lifestyle management can be an effective means to promote better health.

"What does this mean for those of us who are not Seventh-day Adventists?" ask authors Chris Rucker and Jan Hoffman in *The Seventh-Day Diet*. "It means that instead of waiting for science to give us a 'magic pill' for cancer, instead of waiting for more . . . sophisticated types of surgery to control heart disease, instead of cringing at the thought of another painful, self-depriving weight-loss program, we can take a look at the practices of a people who have found a better way."

The *Choices* Eating-Right Plan

The *Choices* lifestyle plan reflects these scientific studies, and emphasizes a plant-based vegetarian diet as the ideal diet to promote glowing good health.

The *Choices* plan is built on eating a moderate amount of good foods such as fruits, vegetables, nuts, whole grains, seeds, legumes. It avoids meat and high-fat animal products. This eating-right plan is hardly a new idea. God's original plan for humanity's diet is shown in Genesis 1:29. "Behold, I have given you every herb bearing seed, . . . and every tree, in the which is the fruit of a tree yielding seed; to you it shall be for meat." After sin God added to the ideal diet the plants of the field (see Genesis 3:18).

I like this quote from a book written more than 100 years ago entitled *The Ministry of Healing*: "Grains, fruits, nuts, and vegetables constitute the diet chosen for us by our Creator. These foods, prepared in as simple and natural a manner as possible, are the most healthful and nourishing. They impart a strength, a power of endurance, and a vigor of intellect that are not afforded by a more complex and stimulating diet" (p. 296).

A vegetarian diet is now being applauded by most doctors and nutritionists. So whether or not you call yourself a vegetarian, learning to eat like one makes sound nutritional sense.

What Do Vegetarians Eat?

There are several different kinds of vegetarians. Some eat meat, poultry, or fish a few times a week or only on special occasions—semi-vegetarians. Some are strict vegetarians—vegans, who consume no animal products like milk, eggs, or cheese; only 4 percent of vegetarians fit this definition. Lacto-ovo vegetarians, the largest vegetarian group, eat no animal flesh, but include milk, milk products, and eggs in their diets.

Old Vegetarian Myths

There are several nutritional concerns that often surface when people are considering the change to a vegetarian diet. About these, Dr. Dean Ornish, a noted nutritionist, says, "I'm puzzled by people's concerns about the nutritional risks of a vegetarian diet, especially when there are so many well-documented risks in the typical high-fat American diet." You need to know what these concerns are and the real truth about them.

"Vegetarians don't get enough calcium." Vegetarians once were believed to be at risk because the calcium and iron in plant foods were thought to be less readily absorbed. Scientists believe this is no longer a concern. Though many Americans do not meet the recommended daily allowances for calcium (800 mg for adults) and iron (15 mg for adult females), most vegetarians do get enough. Calcium comes from dairy products such as milk, cheese, and yogurt, but is also found in equal or greater amounts in beans, broccoli, dried fruit, dark leafy greens, tofu (soybean curd), and in calcium-fortified foods like cereal, soy milk, or tofu milk.

"Vegetarian diets are low in iron." It's true that meat is high in iron, but there are many good sources of iron in the nonmeat world as well—dark leafy vegetables, dried fruit, seeds, dried beans, as well as iron-fortified cereals and breads. It is important to eat these iron-rich foods at the same meal with a food rich in vitamin C such as oranges, green peppers, tomatoes, limes, lemons, or broccoli. Vitamin C helps the body use the iron more efficiently.

"Vegetarians need to 'mix and match' foods carefully in order to get complete proteins." Years ago vegetarians were warned to carefully combine amino acids in grains, legumes, nuts, and seeds to get "complementary" proteins. Experts now say that eating a variety of plant-based food daily provides enough protein. Laborious "mixing and matching" at each meal is not necessary.

How to Make the Transition to a Vegetarian Diet

The problem for most people, even those who like vegetables, is how to eliminate meat, which has been their dietary mainstay. My advice is to find delicious, fun-to-eat, healthful, plant-based meals that the whole family enjoys. Add these meals—one at a time—to the family's preferred list, replacing less-healthful old favorites. Experiment until you find enough delicious low-fat meals to provide a varied and interesting diet. This book is designed to help you do just that. If you jump into the vegetarian diet without having done this, you and your family may become discouraged and begin to crave the old fat-laden family favorites.

What to Do About Fat

Most of us eat too much fat! When we fill up on fat, we're less likely to eat enough of the foods that we need for good nutrition. A high-fat diet, especially one high in animal fat, can lead to heart disease, cancer, diabetes, and obesity.

You've probably heard the recommendation that healthy adults should keep their fat intake to less than 30 per cent of total calories. This recommendation is easy to meet when you focus on at least a day's worth of food, as opposed to individual foods or recipes. What you're eating over the long run is what's important. Focusing on the percentage of fat in a single food or a single meal can be misleading. Sometimes a food is low in fat and calories, which makes the fat percentage look high. Tofu is a good example. A serving of tofu contains 94 calories and 6 grams of fat, which calculates to 57% of the calories coming from fat. This appears to be much too high when compared with the 30% maximum recommendation. However, 6 grams of fat is low. Grams of fat is a more accurate gauge to measure fat content than overall percentage.

Try keeping track of the amount of fat you eat. You may be surprised! Just keep track of the grams of fat you eat. The food labels list grams of fat. To determine the maximum grams of fat for your individual diet, multiply the total calories you consume by .30 (or 30%); then divide that answer by 9 (because there are 9 calories per gram of fat). This gives you the maximum grams of fat you should eat in a day. For example, if you consume 1,600 calories per day, your fat budget would be 53 grams per day.

Monounsaturated and polyunsaturated fats should make up the majority of your fat intake. Saturated fat, primarily from animal fat, and hydrogenated fats have been shown to increase cholesterol levels. Read the labels, and choose foods with the least amount of hydrogenated fat possible.

How to Cook the Good Stuff Right

If you learn to cook whole grains and legumes right, you'll be able to build fantastic healthy meals around them. So here's my short course on what you need to know about grains and legumes–their nutritional value, the types available, and how and where to buy them. I'll give you tips on how to prepare perfect rice, cook delicious beans, and do wonders with tofu.

Experiment With Rice

If you feel sort of half-hearted about rice, chances are you aren't cooking it right. That's not your fault–the instructions given on the back of the bag and in many cookbooks may not be the best way to prepare it.

Once you've learned to make rice that is slightly chewy, with each grain distinct and plump, you'll find a thousand excuses for eating it. You'll see why it is so loved in many ethnic cuisines including Spanish, Italian, Indonesian, Chinese, and Mexican.

Shop in the ethnic section of your supermarket, or in a specialty store, and you'll soon discover that there are many different kinds of rice. Most of us have grown up eating mostly refined long-grain white rice. This kind of rice is prized in the Middle East for pilafs and such. It's fluffier than the short-grain rice preferred by the Japanese. Short-grain rice, on the other hand, has a lightly sweeter flavor and is a little stickier–a big help if you're eating with chopsticks. It's nice to have both long-grain and short-grain on hand, but either way, be sure to use unrefined brown rice; otherwise you'll miss out on full-bodied flavor and a wealth of nutritional benefits.

These aren't your only choices in rice. India's favorite rice, basmati, is increasingly available in the United States and Canada, even in its unrefined state. This long-grain rice has a wonderful flavor and an almost floral fragrance that fills the kitchen while it's cooking. And if wehani rice is available where you live, be sure to try it. It's a specialty whole-grain rice grown in California, bred from basmati seeds, with a taste similar to cracked wheat. Experiment with the different varieties of rice, and you'll soon get your own sense of which to use.

Making Perfect Rice

No matter what kind of rice you choose, cook it properly. Properly means SLOWLY. The worst thing you can do to rice is to cook it in a lot of water at a full rolling boil. The grains will burst, and you'll end up with a gluey mess and maybe a burned pot.

I have to tell you that the easiest way to make perfect rice is to invest in a rice cooker. Just put the rice and water in the cooker's bowl, 1 part rice to 1 $\frac{1}{4}$ parts water. Or, some cooks, like my friend Chai Mau, just put in the rice and then add water to cover it by about 1 inch. Place the lid on the cooker, push "cook" and you are guaranteed perfect rice every time. The cooker will also keep the rice warm for up to 8 hours. I love to allow the rice to set for several hours after cooking. It seems to taste even better.

If you don't have a rice cooker, choose a heavy pot with a tight-fitting lid. The key is to steam the rice, using a low ratio of water to rice. The directions on the bag usually suggest a ratio of 2 parts water to 1 part rice. This is far too much water. Try adding 1 $\frac{1}{2}$ parts water to 1 part rice and see how well your pot maintains the steam. If you have the right pot, you should be able to get your rice ratio to $1\frac{1}{4}$ parts water to 1 part rice or add just enough water to cover the rice by 1 inch. Your best bet is to experiment. Within a short time you'll have it figured out.

Next, bring the mixture to a rolling boil for 5 minutes or so. Add $\frac{1}{2}$ teaspoon of salt per cup of rice or your favorite seasoning. I like to add $\frac{1}{2}$ teaspoon of George Washington Broth mix (any flavor) or McKay's Chicken seasoning at this point. Cover the pot and reduce the heat to the lowest setting possible. Leave the lid on and don't disturb the rice for 40 minutes to avoid uneven cooking. You can even turn the heat off entirely for the last 10 minutes if the pot is reasonably heavy.

Add variety and character to your rice by toasting it before cooking. Stir it in a dry skillet over medium heat for a few minutes until rice begins to pop. Then add it to the boiling water. The result is a slightly toasted flavor and grains that stay more distinct. Or try sautéing rice in oil or margarine before adding the water. Many pilafs and some Indian recipes specify sautéing onions and spices, then adding the raw rice for a few minutes, and finally the water. This method lets the flavors of the onions and spices penetrate the rice more effectively. Surprise your friends and family by creating your own seasoning combinations.

Lean on Beans

If you're looking for a new way to cut fat in your diet, consider a bean, dried pea, or lentil main dish. These legumes are shown as a meat alternative on the "Eating Right Pyramid," and form a very strong part of the Choices plan. They are good sources of dietary fiber, protein, and minerals, and contain no cholesterol. So lean on them and remember, tofu is also from the legume family, made from soy beans.

In this cookbook, the recipe cooking time is based on using precooked or canned legumes for fix-it-fast 30 minute meals. If you choose to cook your legumes from the dried bean, you'll need to plan ahead to allow for extra soaking and cooking time. (Only lentils and dried split peas do not need to be soaked before cooking.) Read on to learn how to soak beans, determine correct proportions of water to legumes, and select cooking times for different beans.

How to Cook Perfect Beans

First, rinse the dried beans. Then, in a Dutch oven or other large, heavy pot, combine the rinsed beans with cold water (use 8 cups water to 1 pound beans or follow a specified recipe). Bring to a boil. Reduce heat and simmer for 2 minutes. Remove from the heat. Cover and let stand for 1 hour before cooking. Or, if you prefer, omit the simmering; soak the beans in cold water overnight in a covered bowl in the refrigerator. Before cooking, drain and rinse the beans, then follow the cooking directions in the recipe, using the amount of fresh water specified.

Cooking Times for Legumes

Item	Pressure Cooker 10# Pressure	Simmering on Stove Top
Lentils	5-10 minutes	45 minutes
Navy Beans	20 minutes	1 hour
White Lima Beans	30-40 minutes	2-3 hours
Great White N. Beans	30-40 minutes	2-3 hours
Green Split Peas	20 minutes	1 hour
Green Whole Peas	30-45 minutes	3-4 hours
Yellow Split Peas	20 minutes	1 hour
Black-eyed Peas	30 minutes	1-2 hours
Kidney Beans	60 minutes	3-4 hours
Chili Beans	45-60 minutes	3-4 hours
Pinto Beans	60 minutes	3-4 hours
Soy Beans	60-70 minutes	24 hours or more
Garbanzos	60-70 minutes	24 hours or more
Rice (brown), long or short	10-20 minutes	1 hour

All About Tofu

To some, tofu is a brand-new eating adventure. To others, familiar with its honorable 2500-year history, it's a taste delight whose benefits are already evident.

Tofu, also known as bean curd, is made by a process similar to making cheese. Soy milk is curdled by adding a coagulant. The curds are pressed into soft cakes, resulting in a soft custard-like food which is the primary food staple of over one billion people. The only plant-based complete protein, tofu contains all eight essential amino acids. Completely cholesterol-free, tofu is very low in saturated fats and is a nutritious source of unsaturated fats. It is also very low in sodium.

How to Buy and Store Tofu

Tofu comes in varying textures and degrees of firmness. Intended use determines the type to choose. A soft "silken" type is ideal for blending in dressing, sauces, dips, or frostings. Medium-soft is best for puddings, pies, cheesecakes, and salads. Firm and extra firm are easier to handle for slicing, marinating, grilling, and stir-frying. Read the label for a description of the consistency.

Although tofu is often described as tasting bland, flavor does vary, depending on the type of soy bean and coagulant used in processing. Tofu absorbs the flavors of the seasonings used with it. It's worth a little experimentation to find the flavor and consistency you like best in your favorite recipes.

Tofu is sold several ways: water-packed in plastic tubs, vacuum packed, or aseptically packaged. Aseptic packs are airtight cardboard boxes which don't need refrigeration until they're opened. The other packing methods require constant refrigeration from time of manufacture to consumption. Consumers have occasionally had bad experiences with sour or bitter tofu, which has actually spoiled on the grocer's shelves. Generally this problem arises with the traditional method of packaging the processed tofu in water-filled plastic tubs. In some stores, days or even weeks may have passed between the time of manufacture and sale, allowing bacterial growth to occur. So if you have had a bad experience with tofu, don't give up. Be sure to check the expiration date on the package. Fresh tofu has a mild bean odor. Return it to the store if it smells sour or has a strong odor.

Many Oriental shops produce fresh tofu daily. This is my choice. This type is usually soft, like custard. It is more economical and better tasting. Fresh Oriental tofu also has less fat than the American type.

Handle tofu as you would any perishable food. Keep it refrigerated. To keep tofu at its freshest, drain water from the plastic tub daily and cover the tofu with cold water. My friend, Chai, suggests sprinkling the tofu and cold water with a small amount of salt to help preserve it longer. Rinse the block of tofu and add a little more salt each time you change the water. This keeps tofu fresh for up to one week.

If tofu is not used within a week, it may be drained, freezer-wrapped, and frozen for up to six months. To thaw, unwrap and pour boiling water over the tofu and let stand until pliable, about 5 to 15 minutes. Drain and squeeze out excess water. After thawing, tofu's texture will be spongier–more like hamburger. It can be easily crumbled and browned.

How to Cook With Tofu

The recipes in this book are only a sampling of the many culinary delights possible with tofu. Its versatility is endless. Slice it, cube it, blend it, stir-fry it, marinate it, grill it, bake it, broil it, steam it, or do as the Orientals do and just eat it raw. Use it in main dishes, breads, desserts, soups, salads, salad dressings, and dips.

Tofu makes the best dairy and egg substitutes. Look at the many recipes in the variation section for tofu whipped cream, sour cream, mayonnaise, salad dressings, etc.

The *Choices* Plan Is Built on the "Eating Right Pyramid"

Grains, fruits, and vegetables form the foundation of the pyramid, and make up the bulk of a healthful diet. Animal products such as meat, poultry, cheese, and eggs are found in the smaller upper portion of the pyramid, and should be eaten in limited quantities, or eliminated entirely. The key to a healthful vegetarian diet is to consume enough calories to maintain a healthy weight while eating a wide variety of foods. The recipes in this book follow these guidelines.

THE VEGETARIAN FOOD PYRAMID

A DAILY GUIDE TO FOOD CHOICES

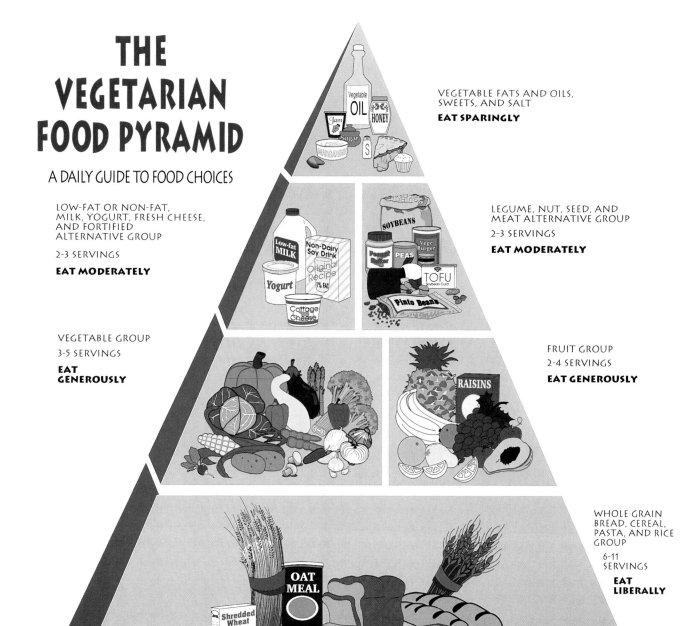

VEGETABLE FATS AND OILS, SWEETS, AND SALT

EAT SPARINGLY

LOW-FAT OR NON-FAT, MILK, YOGURT, FRESH CHEESE, AND FORTIFIED ALTERNATIVE GROUP

2-3 SERVINGS

EAT MODERATELY

LEGUME, NUT, SEED, AND MEAT ALTERNATIVE GROUP

2-3 SERVINGS

EAT MODERATELY

VEGETABLE GROUP

3-5 SERVINGS

EAT GENEROUSLY

FRUIT GROUP

2-4 SERVINGS

EAT GENEROUSLY

WHOLE GRAIN BREAD, CEREAL, PASTA, AND RICE GROUP

6-11 SERVINGS

EAT LIBERALLY

Illustration by Merle Poirier

© The Health Connection, 1994 PRINTED IN USA

Left margin (rotated): Limit foods high in fat, cholesterol, sugar, and salt. | Select relative portions to meet your caloric need. | Choose from a variety of whole grains, fruits, and vegetables.

Food Groups	One Serving Equals One Item	Nutrient Contributions	Calories			Food Choice Examples
			1600 Many Women and Older Adults	**2200** Children, Teen Girls, Active Women, and Most Men	**2800** Teen Boys and Active Men	
Eat Liberally 6-11 Servings daily **Whole Grain Group**	1 slice bread (30 gm) ¹/₂ cup hot cereal (100 gm) 1 cup dry cereal (30 gm) ¹/₄ cup granola (30 gm) ¹/₂ cup rice or pasta (100 gm) 1 tortilla (30 gm) 1 chapati (30 gm) ¹/₂ bagel or English Muffin (30 gm) 3-4 crackers (30 gm) ¹/₂ muffin (30 gm) ¹/₂ cup cooked beans (100 gm)	Complex CHO Fiber Protein Vitamin B₁ (Thiamine) Vitamin B₂ (Riboflavin) Vitamin B₆ and Niacin Iron Magnesium Calcium Trace minerals	6	9	11	Grains: oats, brown rice, barley, millet, bulgar wheat, rye, corn, whole wheat, multi-grain, etc.
Eat Generously 3-5 Servings daily **Vegetable Group**	1 cup raw, leafy vegetable salad (50 gm) ¹/₂ cup chopped raw vegetables (50 gm) ¹/₂ cup cooked vegetables (80 gm) ³/₄ cup vegetable juice (180 gm)	Fiber Potassium Beta-Carotene Folate Vitamin C Calcium Magnesium	3	4	5	Vegetables: broccoli, kale, cabbage, collards, spinach, pumpkin, carrots, winter squash, sweet potatoes, potatoes, parsnips, rutabagas, turnips, tomatoes, beets, eggplant, okra, summer squash, cauliflower
Eat Generously 2-4 Servings daily **Fruit Group**	1 medium, whole fruit (100 gm) ¹/₂ cup canned fruit (125 gm) ¹/₄ cup dried fruit (100 gm) 1 cup berries (100 gm) ³/₄ cup fruit juice (180 gm)	Vitamin C Beta-Carotene Fiber Potassium Folate Magnesium	2	3	4	Fruits: oranges, grapefruit, lemons, apricots, peaches, nectarines, plums, persimmons, apples, pears, kiwi, papaya, mango, pineapple, bananas, strawberries, raspberries, blueberries Dried Fruits: raisins, dates, pears, pineapple, prunes, peaches, figs
Eat Moderately 2-3 Servings daily **Legume, Nut, Seed, and Meat Alternative Group**	¹/₂ cup cooked beans or peas (100 gm) ¹/₂ cup tofu (100 gm) ¹/₄ cup seeds (30 gm) ¹/₄ cup (1 oz.) nuts (30 gm) 2 Tbs (1 oz.) nut butter (30 gm) ¹/₄ cup meat alternative (30 gm) 2 egg whites (50 gm)	Protein Zinc Iron Fiber Calcium Vitamin B₆ Vitamin E Niacin (B₃) Linoelic Acid	2	2-3	3	Legumes: pinto, black, white, navy, soybeans, garbanzoes, lentils, blackeye, green pea, split pea, peanuts Nuts: almonds, walnuts, filberts, chestnuts, brazil, pecans, cashews Seed: pine nuts, sesame, sunflower, pumpkin Alternatives: tofu, meat alternatives
Eat Moderately 2-3 Servings daily **Low-Fat Dairy Group**	1 cup milk, nonfat or lowfat (245 gm) 1 cup soymilk (fortified) (245 gm) ¹/₂ cup lowfat cottage cheese (100 gm) ¹/₂ cup soy cheese (100 gm) 1 ¹/₂ oz. fresh cheese (45 gm) 1 cup low-fat or non-fat yogurt (225 gm) 1 Tbs (¹/₂ oz.) cream cheese (15 gm)	Calcium Protein Vitamins A and D Riboflavin (B₂) Vitamin B₁₂	2	2-3	3	Dairy: milk, yogurt, cottage cheese, ricotta, other fresh cheeses Fortified Alternatives: soy or tofu milk, soy cheese

Eat Sparingly **Vegetable Fats and Oils, Sweets, and Salt**	The small tip of the Pyramid shows vegetable fats and oils, salt, and sweets. These foods such as salad dressings and vegetable oils, cream, butter, margarine, sour cream, cream cheese, sugars, soft drinks, candies, and sweet desserts provide calories and are low in nutrients. Vegetable oils contain essential fatty acids, but use these sparingly because they are high in calories. For every tablespoon of fat added to a 2200 calorie diet, you increase the percentage of calories as fat by approximately five percent. Every tablespoon of sugar adds two percent calories as sugar.

- Use visible fats sparingly.
- Limit desserts to two or three per week.
- Use honey, jams, jelly, corn syrups, molasses, sugar sparingly.
- Use soft drinks and candies very sparingly, if at all.
- Limit foods high in salt.

1 Tbs margarine	= 11.4 gm fat	102 calories	0 mg. cholesterol
1 Tbs butter	= 12.0 gm fat	108 calories	33 mg. cholesterol
1 Tbs mayonnaise	= 11.0 gm fat	99 calories	4 mg. cholesterol
1 Tbs sour cream	= 3.0 gm fat	30 calories	5 mg. cholesterol
1 Tbs cream cheese	= 5.0 gm fat	52 calories	15 mg. cholesterol
1 Tbs cream	= 15.0 gm fat	52 calories	21 mg. cholesterol
1 Tbs sugar	= 12 gm	48 calories	
1 tsp sugar	= 4 gm	16 calories	
1 Tbs honey	= 21 gm	64 calories	

1 tsp salt (5 gm table salt) = 2000 mg sodium
1 Tbs oil = 13.6 gm fat 120.0 calories
1 tsp oil = 4.5 gm fat 40.1 calories

EGG TORTILLA
This low-cholesterol
meal is the perfect choice
for brunch.

Recipe on page 29

Nutritious Breakfast Ideas With Fix-It-Fast Ease

We've changed the way we eat dinner and desserts, so why begin the day with the same old foods? Blame it on the time pressures or the fact we are not quite awake, but breakfast menus are often the least imaginative of the day. They don't need to be that way!

No Food Needs to Be Off Limits at Breakfast!

Take a tip from breakfast menus around the world. Other cultures don't limit their morning fare. The Japanese often have soup for breakfast, the Chinese like rice, steamed or fried, and Mexicans enjoy tacos or enchiladas early in the morning. So expand your horizons at breakfast.

Mom Was Right!

Our mothers have been telling us for years that a "good" breakfast is important. Recent medical studies have backed up Mom's commonsense advice not to skip breakfast with some pretty compelling reasons. Starting the day with nutritious, particularly fiber-rich, foods may be linked to lower cholesterol levels, greater ability to concentrate, more energy and endurance, better weight control, and even longevity.

Breakfast should provide a minimum of one fourth of the day's total calories. Nutritionists recommend that 60 percent of these calories come from complex carbohydrates, the kind found in whole-grain breads, cereals, pasta, rice, and beans.

Eating healthier breakfasts can save you money. Breakfast cereals are getting more and more expensive. Read on for recipes that provide healthful and inexpensive alternatives, even on those busy mornings when the whole family is on the run.

Be sure to look for the nondairy version for many of these recipes. They are just as tasty, and very nutritious! Who could say no to a **Granola and Fruit Parfait**? **Toasted Muesli** adds a delicious European flare for breakfast. **Spiced Oatmeal with Fruit and Nuts** is a great way to lower cholesterol. A **Strawberry-Banana Yogurt Smoothie** provides plenty of calcium and vitamin C. And all of them are quick to make, healthy to eat, and delicious!

When the morning isn't quite as rushed, entice your family to the kitchen with simple variations on traditional favorites: **Light 'n Fruity Pancakes, Garden Vegetable Egg Tortillas,** or an **Italian Frittata.**

You can keep calories from fats and sugars under control. Watch those doughnuts, sweet rolls, calorie-laden syrups, and high-sugar dry cereals! Instead, take advantage of the sweetness of fruit, and offer your family a delicious yet healthy way to satisfy a morning craving for sweets.

When breakfast is "on the run," this Granola and Fruit Parfait will help hold you over until lunch.

GRANOLA AND FRUIT PARFAIT

Serves 1

Preparation time: 5 minutes

M E N U   T I P S

This breakfast brings together the sweetness of fresh fruit and cream and the crunch of toasted grains. This recipe also makes a delicious, low-fat dessert. Replace the granola with Grape-Nuts cereal for a refreshing change.
For a special brunch treat, layer the mixtures in a large glass bowl.

D O - A H E A D   T I P S

Make granola ahead of time. If you are making the nondairy parfait version, you can make the Tofu Whipped Cream several days ahead. The fruit may be cut up the night before, but assemble the parfait just before serving so the granola does not get soggy.

$^2/_3$ Cup assorted fresh fruits, such as melons, oranges, pineapple, kiwi, berries, apples, *or* seedless grapes, cut into $^1/_2$-inch chunks.

$^1/_4$ - $^1/_2$ Cup low- *or* nonfat plain, vanilla, *or* lemon-flavored yogurt (for the nondairy version replace yogurt with equal amounts of tofu whipped cream. Recipe is in the nondairy variation section in the back of the book.)

4   Tablespoons granola (see recipe following *or* use purchased granola)

❶ Place a third of the fruit in the bottom of a parfait glass or goblet, reserving a few choice pieces for garnish, and top with 2-4 tablespoons of yogurt *or* tofu whipped cream, and 2 tablespoons of granola.

❷ Repeat the layers, ending with yogurt *or* tofu whipped cream.

❸ Garnish with reserved fruit.

> A palate-pleasing blend of flavors and textures — this breakfast is pretty enough for company.

> 🍃
> This fruit sweetened version is adapted from my mom's recipe. How well I remember the smell of granola baking in her kitchen!
> 🍃

GRANOLA

Makes 11 cups or 22 servings
Preparation time: 15 minutes
Baking time: 1 ½ hours

RECIPE TIPS

For a sweeter taste, add honey to the liquid ingredients, or brown sugar to the dry ingredients. I prefer a lighter-tasting granola sweetened only with apple juice concentrate and dates. Maple flavoring adds an interesting taste. Experiment to find the taste that is just right for you. Be sure to bake the granola until it is nicely toasted and light brown in color. With the addition of milk and fresh fruit, you have a nutritionally balanced breakfast on the run.

7	Cups oats, rolled *or* quick
1 ½	Cups toasted wheat germ
1	Cup nuts (almonds, pecans, walnuts, *or* any combination), slivered *or* chopped
1 ¼	Cups coconut, sweetened *or* unsweetened
1	Teaspoon salt
1	Cup frozen apple juice concentrate
¼ - ½	Cup dates, pitted (optional)
½	Cup oil
2	Teaspoons pure vanilla extract
½	Teaspoon pure almond extract
⅛	Teaspoon maple flavoring (optional)
½	Cup dried fruit (dates, raisins, apricots, etc.), chopped *or* whole

❶ Mix first 5 ingredients in large gallon-sized bowl.

❷ Combine liquid ingredients in separate bowl, mixing well. (For a sweeter granola, put the apple juice concentrate in a blender, add ¼ to ½ cup dates, and blend until liquefied. Then add the remaining liquid ingredients and mix well.)

❸ Add liquid mixture to dry ingredient mixture, a little at a time, mixing thoroughly after each addition of liquid.

❹ Spread mixture thinly—no more than 1 inch thick—on large cookie sheets. Bake at 225 to 250° F for 1 ½ hours, stirring every half hour. Watch carefully, and adjust temperature if granola is browning too quickly or is not lightly toasted after 1 ½ hours.

❺ Sprinkle on chopped, dried fruit of choice during last 10 minutes of baking and continue baking until the fruit is just softened.

❻ Remove from oven and toss the warm granola to mix in the dried fruit. Let cool and place in airtight container. Store in the refrigerator or freezer. You can make large amounts of granola because it will keep in airtight containers in the freezer for several months.

STRAWBERRY-BANANA BREAKFAST SMOOTHIE

Makes 2 $\frac{1}{2}$ cups or 2 servings
Preparation time: 5 minutes

R E C I P E   T I P S

You can make this smoothie with any fruit combination you choose. The bananas give a nice smooth consistency and flavor to any other fruit you combine with them. Try both the yogurt and the tofu option. There is very little difference in taste. The tofu takes on whatever flavor you add to it and has the same smooth consistency as yogurt.

❖

Yogurt Option:

1	Cup fresh strawberries *or* individually frozen strawberries, slightly thawed
1	Medium banana, cut in slices
$\frac{1}{2}$	Cup nonfat milk
1	8-ounce carton strawberry lowfat yogurt

❶ In blender container, combine all ingredients.

❷ Cover; blend at medium speed 30 - 60 seconds or until smooth. Serve immediately.

Nondairy Smoothie:

1	Cup fresh strawberries *or* individually frozen strawberries, slightly thawed
1	Medium banana, cut in slices
$\frac{1}{2}$	Cup low-fat tofu milk, cold
1	Cup soft tofu, drained
$\frac{1}{4}$	Teaspoon pure vanilla extract (preferably white vanilla for color)
$\frac{1}{4}$	Teaspoon lemon juice
	Honey to desired sweetness (optional)

❶ In blender container, combine all ingredients.

❷ Cover; blend at medium speed 30 - 60 seconds or until smooth. Serve immediately.

A sweet and creamy way to start the day!

MUESLI

Makes about 8 cups or 16 servings
Preparation time: 15 minutes
Cooking time: 30 minutes

M E N U   T I P S

Muesli is a Swiss word meaning "mush," but it is usually eaten as a cold cereal. Use whatever combination of fruit and nuts you like. Pour milk or fruit juice over the muesli and serve with a piece of fresh fruit or a glass of juice for a complete breakfast.

D O - A H E A D   T I P S

Nuts and rolled oats can be toasted several days ahead of assembly time.

❖

5	Cups rolled oats
2	Teaspoons cinnamon (optional)
$\frac{1}{4}$	Cup whole hazelnuts or pecan halves
$\frac{1}{2}$	Cup sliced almonds
$\frac{1}{2}$	Cup toasted wheat germ
$\frac{1}{2}$	Cup dried apricots, sliced
$\frac{1}{2}$	Cup dried cranberries
$\frac{1}{2}$	Cup golden raisins
$\frac{1}{2}$	Cup dried apple slices
$\frac{1}{2}$	Cup nonfat milk *or* tofu milk

❶ Heat oven to 375° F. Mix oats with cinnamon and spread on a baking sheet. Toast for 15 minutes.

❷ Toast hazelnuts until skins loosen, about 10 minutes. Rub off skins and chop coarsely. Or toast pecan halves for about 4 minutes. Toast almonds for about 4 minutes.

❸ Combine toasted nuts with toasted oats, wheat germ, and dried fruit. Toss together and place in an airtight jar. Muesli will keep for several weeks. Serve with hot or cold nonfat milk *or* tofu milk.

The flavors of dried fruit and toasted nuts and oats combine to create a mouthwatering, European favorite, breakfast cereal.

CORNMEAL HEARTS AND STARS

Serves 6
Preparation time: 5 minutes
Cooking time: 10 minutes
Cooling time: 5-10 minutes

M E N U   T I P S

This is a wonderful way to get your children to eat cooked cereal. Let them help put the corn-meal mush into the molds, or if you don't have molds handy, spoon the cornmeal out onto a plate in a circular shape and let the kids put dried fruit and fresh fruit on top to make a face or any other designs they like. Serve the cornmeal stars with fresh fruit and whole-grain toast for a complete breakfast.

D O - A H E A D   T I P S

You can make a large amount of these cornmeal shapes and keep them covered in the refriger-ator for up to a week. Just reheat in microwave for about 30 seconds or until warm.

◆

$^3/_4$ Cup cornmeal (white *or* yellow)

$^3/_4$ Cup cold water

$2\,^1/_2$ Cups boiling water

$^3/_4$ Teaspoon salt

Raspberry Sauce:

3   Cups fresh *or* frozen raspberries

❶ Mix cornmeal and cold water in saucepan. (If you have a mill and enjoy milling your own grain, try the unbeatable taste of freshly milled popcorn in this recipe.)

❷ Stir in boiling water and salt.

❸ Cook, stirring constantly, until mixture thickens and boils; reduce heat. Cover and simmer on very low for 10 minutes.

❹ Spray mold, corn bread pan, or whatever container you are using with non-stick vegetable spray. Pour the hot cornmeal into the molds. Let cool in the refrigerator until the cornmeal thickens enough to hold its shape (5-10 minutes).

❺ While the cornmeal shapes are cooling, place the raspberries (thawed if using frozen) in a blender container and whiz until well blended. Pour blended raspberries into sieve to strain out seeds.

❻ To assemble: On individual serving plates, pour approximately $^1/_3$ cup of raspberry sauce. Turn plate to spread sauce evenly. Place warm cornmeal shapes on bed of raspberry sauce. (Cornmeal shapes can be reheated in microwave for 30 seconds if too cool.) You can also serve them topped with applesauce, peach sauce (peaches with juice blended), or honey.

FRUIT TOAST

Serves 4
Preparation time: 5 minutes
Cooking time: 5-8 minutes

RECIPE TIPS

This recipe may be made with any cooked fruit (apricots, pears, peaches, berries, etc.). Applesauce and other fairly thick fruit purees need only be heated without further thickening. Or you can use dried fruits soaked or cooked in fruit juice and blended. Just add enough fruit juice to make a sauce to pour over the toast. Our favorite juices to use in these fruit sauces are apple and pineapple. Grape juice works with blueberries or other dark fruits. Cranberry juice is delicious with raspberries and strawberries. This sauce is also great served over pancakes, waffles, or French toast.

◆

3	Cups cooked fruit
1 $^1/_2$	Cups fruit juice
	Honey to sweeten (optional)
1 $^1/_2$	Tablespoons cornstarch
4	Slices whole wheat toast

❶ Bring fruit, mashed slightly, cubed, sliced, *or* whole, to a boil in fruit juice.

❷ Moisten cornstarch with an equal amount of cold water, stirring until the cornstarch is dissolved. Stir into boiling fruit mixture.

❸ Bring fruit mixture to a boil, lower temperature and cook for approximately 3 minutes, stirring occasionally. Serve over toast spread with margarine *or* peanut butter. Or spoon over toast and top with a little yogurt *or* Tofu Whipped Cream. (Recipe in variation section of book.)

> ❧
> This was my favorite breakfast when I was growing up. Mom used home-canned peaches and homemade whole-wheat bread.
> ☙

SPICED OATMEAL WITH FRUIT AND NUTS

Serves 2
Preparation time: 5 minutes
Cooking time: 10 minutes

RECIPE TIPS

Get creative with your oatmeal! Add chopped apple and dates to the oats during cooking for a different taste treat. Use any variety of dried fruit in place of or in addition to the dates, or replace the apple with other fresh fruits.

◆

1 $^1/_2$	Cups water
$^1/_4$	Teaspoon ground cinnamon (optional)
$^1/_8$	Teaspoon salt
$^2/_3$	Cup regular rolled oats
$^1/_2$	Small apple, chopped
2	Tablespoons pitted whole dates, chopped
1	Tablespoon sliced almonds
1 $^1/_2$	Teaspoons brown sugar *or* honey
1 $^1/_3$	Cups nonfat milk *or* tofu milk

❶ Combine water, cinnamon, and salt in a medium saucepan. Bring to boiling; stir in oats. Cook for 5 minutes, stirring occasionally. Let stand, covered, till of desired consistency.

❷ Divide oatmeal mixture between two serving bowls. Top each bowl of oatmeal with some chopped apple, chopped dates, sliced almonds, and brown sugar *or* honey to sweeten. Divide milk between two serving bowls.

Oats have been found to lower cholesterol levels, another good reason to eat your oatmeal!

ITALIAN FRITTATA

Serves 4-6

Preparation time: 10 minutes
Cooking time: 5 minutes
Baking time: 20 minutes, low-fat dairy option
Baking time: 30 minutes, nondairy option

M E N U   T I P S

A cholesterol-free breakfast with a low-fat dairy and a nondairy option, this recipe still preserves the tradition and flavor of eggs for breakfast. Serve this delicious breakfast main dish with whole-grain toast and fresh fruit for a balanced meal.

◆

1	Tablespoon olive oil *or* 3 tablespoons water
1	Large onion, thinly sliced
2	Medium zucchini, thinly sliced
$^1/_2$	Red pepper, chopped
$^1/_4$	Cup fresh parsley, chopped
4	Fresh garlic cloves, pressed *or* chopped fine
$^1/_2$	Teaspoon dried oregano *or* 1 teaspoon chopped fresh oregano
$^1/_2$	Teaspoon dried basil *or* 1 teaspoon chopped fresh oregano
$^1/_8$	Teaspoon salt (optional)
$^3/_4$	Cup tomato sauce to top each finished serving of frittata (optional)

Low-fat Dairy Option:

2	Cups Morningstar Farms Better 'n Eggs® *or* egg whites
1	Tablespoon nonfat milk *or* nondairy milk
2	Tablespoons flour
$^1/_2$	Teaspoon salt (optional)
$^1/_2$	Teaspoon garlic powder

Nondairy Option:

1 $^1/_2$	Cups *or* $^3/_4$ Pound soft tofu, blended
$^1/_2$	Cup *or* $^1/_4$ Pound soft tofu, mashed
4	Tablespoon flour
1	Teaspoon salt
$^1/_2$	Teaspoon garlic powder
1	Tablespoons light soy sauce (optional)

❶ In nonstick skillet or 10-inch cast-iron skillet, sauté in oil or steam covered with water, onions, zucchini, and red pepper just until tender. Add parsley, garlic, oregano, basil, and salt and steam or sauté an additional minute. Remove from heat and set aside.

Dairy Option

❶ In separate bowl whip egg whites *or* Better 'n Eggs with 1 tablespoon of nonfat milk. Add flour, if desired, salt, and garlic powder and mix well.

❷ In 10-inch cast-iron skillet or baking dish sprayed with vegetable spray, place the sautéed vegetable mixture. Top with the egg mixture and bake in a 450° F oven until eggs are set and the sides have puffed, about 20 minutes. Reduce the oven temperature if eggs cook too fast. The top should be golden brown and a knife inserted in the middle should come out clean. Do not overcook. The frittata should be firm but not dry. Top each serving with tomato sauce if desired.

This Italian Frittata is an omelette-like, one-dish breakfast entrée!

Nondairy Option:

❶ In blender container blend 1 $^1/_2$ cups soft tofu, adding a very small amount of water only if necessary to run blender. The firmer the tofu, the more water you will need to add. Mash the additional $^1/_2$ cup of tofu coarsely. Add salt, garlic powder, flour, baking powder, and soy sauce and mix well. Add sautéed vegetables to tofu mixture and mix well.

❷ Spray a large 10-inch cast-iron skillet with vegetable spray, coating well. Pour all the above mixture into the skillet. Bake at 400° F for 15 minutes on one side, flip and bake 15 minutes more, or until golden brown. Make smaller frittatas by pouring $^1/_2$ cupfuls onto sprayed baking sheet. Flatten each mound into a circle. Bake at 400° F for 15 minutes on one side, flip and bake 10 minutes more or until golden brown. Do not overcook. Frittatas should be firm but not dry. Top each serving with tomato sauce if desired.

Kids and adults alike will love these healthy, whole-grain pancakes.

LIGHT 'N FRUITY OAT PANCAKES

Serves 6
Preparation time: 5 minutes
Cooking time: 15 minutes

R E C I P E   T I P S

This dish may also be served with the fruit sauce from the fruit toast recipe. This fruit topping provides a sweet taste with a lot less sugar and calories and a lot more vitamins and minerals than maple syrup! This recipe also makes great Belgian or regular waffles. Although rice flour or unbleached flour makes a lighter pancake, you can vary the recipe by using whole-wheat flour.

Either way, be sure to wait for the yeast to leaven the batter for 5-8 minutes. Serve these pancakes with fruit cream and fresh fruit on the side for a complete breakfast.

D O - A H E A D   T I P S

You can make these pancakes ahead of time and freeze for last-minute mornings. Just individually wrap and freeze. Thaw and warm in the microwave or toaster oven.

◆

1	Cup rice flour *or* unbleached flour
$3/4$	Cup whole-wheat flour
$2\ 3/4$	Cups warm tofu milk *or* water
3	Tablespoons honey
2	Teaspoons yeast
$1\ 1/2$	Teaspoons salt
$1/8$	Cup almonds
$1/8$	Cup raw sesame seeds (optional)
$1\ 3/4$	Cups oats

❶ Put everything except oats in blender and blend on high until smooth. Be sure the liquid is warm so that the yeast can begin leavening immediately.

❷ Add oats through top while blender is going until motor will not handle any more batter. (Stop even if all of oats have not been used. Do not add more.) Let sit for 5 to 8 minutes to activate yeast.

❸ Heat griddle on medium heat until hot. Pour enough batter to form about 4 inch or 5 inch pancakes. Cook each pancake until top starts to dry. Flip over and brown other side.

❹ Serve topped with fruited cream (recipe following).

Trish Hayden shared this recipe with me. Trish is an artist and photographer who loves to invent healthful and delicious meals.

This dish also makes a great light lunch or supper.

FRUITED CREAM

Serves 6

Preparation time: 5 minutes

M E N U   T I P S

The Tofu Whipped Cream can be replaced with any commercial low-fat whipped topping alternative.

D O - A H E A D   T I P S

The whipped topping can be made ahead of time and folded into the fruit just before serving.

---

1 ½ Cups fresh, frozen and partially thawed, or cooked fruit (strawberries, raspberries, blackberries, blueberries, crushed pineapple, grated apple, apricot puree, cubed bananas, etc.)

1 ½ Cups whipped chilled evaporated nonfat milk flavored with vanilla and sweetened with honey (optional)

or 1 ½ Cups **Tofu Whipped Cream** (recipe in variation section of book)

❶ Select fruit *or* fruit combination and chop, cut into small pieces, puree, *or* mash your fruit, depending on the type of fruit chosen and your preferences.

❷ Prepare the evaporated whipped topping *or* the tofu whipped topping.

❸ Fold the fruit into the whipped topping of choice. Chill and serve over pancakes, waffles, French toast, desserts, etc.

GARDEN VEGETABLE EGG TORTILLAS

Serves 6
Preparation time: 15 minutes
Cooking time: 15 minutes

M E N U   T I P S

Vary the vegetables in this recipe. Try adding broccoli or carrots for a mid-morning brunch. This one-dish breakfast includes foods from the vegetable group, bread group, and meat alternative group—brought together to provide a balanced meal. Prosage Breakfast Links come frozen, and may be purchased at many health food stores. Garnish this dish with a slice of fresh fruit.

◆

6	(8-inch) flour tortillas
2	Cups (2 medium) zucchini, thinly sliced
2	Cups fresh mushrooms, sliced
$^1/_2$	Cup green peppers, chopped
4	Worthington Prosage® Links, thawed and sliced
$^1/_4$	Cup green onions, sliced
1	Medium tomato, diced (1 cup)
3	Teaspoons or to taste, hot or mild salsa *or* picante sauce
$^1/_2$	Teaspoon diced basil leaves
$^1/_4$	Teaspoon garlic powder
$^1/_4$	Teaspoon salt (optional)
12	Egg whites
or 1 $^1/_2$	Cups Morningstar Farms Better 'n Eggs®
or 1 $^1/_2$	Cups firm tofu drained and mashed
	Salsa to garnish

❶ Warm tortillas, covered, in oven on low temperature.

❷ In large nonstick skillet sprayed with nonstick vegetable spray, combine zucchini, mushrooms, green peppers, and Worthington Prosage Links. Cook over medium-high heat until crisp-tender.

❸ Add onions, tomato, salsa, basil, garlic powder, and salt.

❹ Cover; reduce heat to medium. Cook 1 to 2 minutes or until tomato is thoroughly heated. Remove from pan. Cover; keep warm.

❺ Spray large nonstick skillet with nonstick vegetable spray. Beat Better 'n Eggs and pour eggs into skillet. (If using egg whites, beat with 2 tablespoons of water before pouring into skillet.) Cook over medium heat until eggs are firm but moist, stirring frequently.

For nondairy option:
Use firm tofu, drained and mashed. Place in nonstick skillet and lightly brown. Add extra garlic powder and salt to taste if desired. Tofu has no flavor and it needs a little more seasoning than eggs. Also, you may add turmeric to give tofu a yellow color. McKay's Chicken-Style Seasoning also gives extra flavor to the tofu and imitates the yellow color of eggs. Stir tofu until brown.

❻ Add egg *or* tofu mixture to vegetable mixture. Spoon onto center of tortillas; roll up. Serve immediately, garnished with salsa.

Pictured on page 16

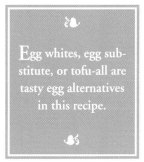

Egg whites, egg substitute, or tofu-all are tasty egg alternatives in this recipe.

L U N C H

CIRCULAR SUB
Make this casual, hearty sandwich for your next tailgate picnic.

Recipe on page 41

Add nutritious fuel to power up your lunch menus

Lunchtime finds most family members away from home, either on the job or at school. Whether you eat out at lunchtime or "brown-bag it," lunch seems to be the least-planned meal of the day.

You may be tempted to grab anything that's fast.

It's noon. Both the clock on the wall and your stomach tell you it's time to find something—anything—to eat! It's so easy to run to the nearest fast-food restaurant and grab a burger, fries, and shake. But if you're trying to eat healthier, you could be in for a surprise. That burger-and-fries lunch could add up to almost 1,200 calories, with half coming from fat. And if you're hoping to add more fiber to your diet, you'd better look elsewhere!

Lunch is a meal — not just a snack!

Are you responsible for packing the family lunch boxes? Because of lack of time, you may be tempted to throw in a jelly sandwich on white bread, some potato chips, a soft drink, and a cookie. This meal will provide one third of the calories needed for the day, as lunch should, but it comes up short in the nutrient department. Not to mention the fact that it is shockingly high in fat and sugar, and low in fiber.

You need a "power lunch"!

Whether it's in a bag, a Snoopy lunch box, eaten at home, or served at a fancy restaurant, you and everyone in your family deserve a delicious lunch that is high in fiber, low in calories and fat, and packed with nutrients.

If you're watching your weight—and so many of us are—a good lunch will help you make it to dinner without overindulging in sweet, high-fat snacks.

So what's a busy person to do for lunch?

Believe it or not, it needn't take a lot of time to prepare a healthful homemade alternative to the usual fast-food fix. A little weekend planning can help you and your whole family eat nutritious lunches all week and still maintain taste appeal.

The latest government-issued dietary guidelines recommend we eat three to five servings of vegetables and two to four servings of fruits every day. That might sound like a lot if you're accustomed to eating them only as a side dish at dinner or supper. Lunchtime offers a good opportunity to get more fruits and vegetables in your diet. Fruits and vegetables can make lunchtime more interesting as well as healthier.

Whole-grain breads can be part of a quick and nutritious lunch, too. Try multigrain breads and rolls. Make your sandwich on a whole-wheat bagel or English muffin. Try pita bread or a tortilla for something out of the ordinary.

Add carrot, celery, or cucumber sticks, or a bowl of melon chunks or peaches to your lunch entrée, rather than the usual potato chips and cookies. Raw fruit and vegetables add a delicious flavor, and the crunch helps satisfy the All-American desire for chips or fries to go with every sandwich.

Part One: The Portable Lunch

This section is devoted to recipes that can be used in brown-bag lunches for kids and adults.
Many can be prepared the night before to ease your busy morning schedule.

PEANUT BUTTER SURPRISE

Serves 1
Preparation time: 5 minutes

R E C I P E   T I P S

This sandwich can be varied with many fruit combinations—banana, apple,
dried fruits—but I think red or green seedless grapes are the best of all. Each
bite produces an unexpected squirt of delicious, sweet juice.
Kids love to prepare this sandwich themselves.

D O - A H E A D   T I P S

Make this sandwich the night before and refrigerate until morning. It can be
eaten straight from the refrigerator or at room temperature.

◆

2	Slices whole-wheat bread
2	Tablespoons peanut butter
20	Whole red *or* green seedless grapes

❶ Spread 1 tablespoon of peanut butter on each slice of bread.

❷ Place whole *or* halved grapes on top of peanut butter on one
piece of bread.

❸ Top with remaining slice of bread and peanut butter.

❹ For a brown-bag lunch, wrap the sandwich tightly in plastic
wrap.

Peanut butter lovers
young and old, this one's
for you. You may never go
back to jelly!

LUNCH BOX BURRITOS

Serves 1
Preparation time: 5 minutes
Cooking time: 2 minutes

R E C I P E   T I P S

This is a favorite among kids and adults alike. For a brown-bag lunch, take
the salsa in a separate container. Make burritos to your own taste, of course.
You control how hot or mild they are—or if you want a nondairy or cheese
version. Vegetarian chili adds a wonderful taste—a change from refried
beans or chili beans. It can be purchased in most health food stores and some
supermarkets. For lunch at home, you can top the burrito with salsa, guacamole, lettuce, and tomatoes and have a Mexican feast. Olé!

D O - A H E A D   T I P S

Make these burritos ahead and freeze in an airtight container.
They'll keep for several months.

◆

	1	Flour tortilla
	$^1/_2$ - 1	Cup Worthington *or* Natural Touch® Vegetarian Chili
	1	Tablespoon hot *or* mild salsa
	2	Tablespoons low-fat mozzarella cheese, grated
or	2	Tablespoons soy cheese, grated
	1	Tablespoon black olives, halves *or* slices

❶ Place 1 flour tortilla on a plate and pour the vegetarian chili
down the center. Top with salsa, cheese of choice, and black
olives.

❷ Fold the bottom side up about 2 inches and then roll the tortilla up from one side. Wrap tightly in plastic wrap and store
in refrigerator or freezer. To serve, unwrap one end of burrito and microwave on high for approximately 2 minutes, or
unwrap completely and bake in oven on cookie sheet until
center is hot.

WALDORF "CHICKEN" SALAD PITAS

Serves 8-10
Preparation time: 10 minutes

R E C I P E   T I P S

This vegetarian version of traditional chicken salad is made with Worthington FriChik®, a delicious soy-based chicken substitute. FriChik comes in a can, and can be purchased in most natural food stores and some supermarkets. For a brown-bag lunch, put the salad in an airtight container and keep cool. Pack pita halves separately and assemble sandwich just before eating. This also makes a delicious main dish salad, served on a bed of lettuce with the pita bread on the side. To vary, replace chopped apple with mandarin oranges, and use pecans or walnuts instead of almonds.

D O - A H E A D   T I P S

Prepare salad up to 3 days before serving and refrigerate.

◆

10	Whole-wheat pita halves
2	Cups Worthington Vegetarian FriChik, coarsely chopped
$1/2$	Cup celery, thinly sliced
1	Cup apple, coarsely chopped
1	Cup seedless red grapes, halved
$1/2$	Cup slivered almonds, walnuts, *or* pecans
$1/2$	Cup scallions, chopped (optional)
$1/2$	Cup water chestnuts, chopped (optional)
	Alfalfa sprouts to garnish

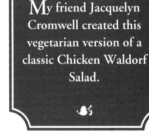

My friend Jacquelyn Cromwell created this vegetarian version of a classic Chicken Waldorf Salad.

Dressing:

$1 1/2$	Cups low-fat mayonnaise, low-fat plain yogurt, *or* **Tofu Whipped Cream** (recipe in variation section)
2	Tablespoons honey *or* sugar
2	Tablespoons lemon juice
1	Teaspoon onion powder (optional)

❶ In large bowl, combine all salad ingredients.

❷ In small bowl, combine all dressing ingredients, mix well.

❸ Pour dressing over salad; toss gently to coat. Refrigerate until serving time.

❹ Place salad in whole-wheat pita halves. Garnish with alfalfa sprouts and serve.

GARBANZO DELIGHT SANDWICH

Serves 6
Preparation time: 15 minutes
Cooking time: 5 minutes

R E C I P E   T I P S

For a brown-bag lunch, make sandwich with two slices of bread. Add everything but the tomatoes and wrap securely in plastic wrap. Put tomatoes in separate container and add just before eating. The vegetarian, cholesterol-free "smoked turkey" is a delicious addition to this sandwich. This product comes frozen, and is available at most health food stores and some supermarkets.

D O - A H E A D   T I P S

The bean spread can be made ahead of time and refrigerated for up to one week.

◆

$1/2$	Cup chopped onion
1	Small garlic clove, minced
2	Tablespoons water
1	(15 ounce) Can garbanzo beans, drained
1	Tablespoon light mayonnaise *or* soft tofu
1	Teaspoon lime juice
6	Slices pumpernickel *or* multigrain bread
2	Cups lettuce, shredded
12	Slices tomato
6	Slices Worthington Vegetarian Smoked "Turkey" (optional)
1	Cup alfalfa sprouts
1	Cup carrots, peeled and shredded

❶ In small nonstick skillet, cook onion and garlic in 2 tablespoons water until onion is tender and water has evaporated.

❷ In blender container, combine onion mixture, beans, mayonnaise *or* tofu, and lime juice; process until smooth and of spreading consistency. Season with garlic powder *or* salt if desired.

❸ Spread bean mixture on bread; top with lettuce, 2 tomato slices, 1 slice of Worthington Smoked Turkey, and sprouts. Sprinkle with carrots and serve.

This protein-filled sandwich is definitely a "power lunch" that will hold you till dinner.

This Avocado Sunshine sandwich is a juicy delight. Serve with lots of napkins.

AVOCADO SUNSHINE

Serves 1

Preparation time: 10 minutes

R E C I P E   T I P S

For a brown-bag lunch, place the avocado in a sealed container and sprinkle with lime or lemon juice to prevent discoloring. Put tomatoes in a sealed plastic bag or container and keep cool. Assemble sandwich just before eating. Vary this sandwich by adding other vegetables. Green leaf lettuce can replace the alfalfa sprouts. Red pepper makes a great addition. Serve with carrot or other vegetable sticks.

D O - A H E A D   T I P S

The vegetables can be cut up ahead of time.

◆

2	Slices whole-wheat or multigrain bread *or* whole-wheat pita bread
¹/₂	Avocado, peeled, seeded, and sliced
¹/₂	Large tomato, sliced thick
¹/₂	Cucumber, peeled and sliced
¹/₂	Cup alfalfa sprouts
1	Tablespoon green onions, chopped (optional)
2	Tablespoons low-fat mayonnaise
or 2	Tablespoons nondairy mayonnaise from variation section
	Garlic powder to taste
	Dried oregano to taste

❶ Spread mayonnaise on each slice of the bread *or* inside pita bread. Sprinkle with garlic powder and oregano to taste.

❷ On one slice of bread layer avocado slices, thick tomato slices, cucumber slices, alfalfa sprouts, and green onions. Top with remaining slice of bread. Serve.

This California-style sandwich will make any day seem bright and sunny!

Talk about healthy and delicious! This recipe combines whole-grain rice, fruits, and nuts with a wonderful low-fat dressing to make an unforgettable sandwich.

BROWN RICE CITRUS SALAD SANDWICH

Serves 6-8

Preparation time: 15 minutes
Cooking time (for rice): 35-40 minutes

R E C I P E T I P S

For a brown-bag lunch, place the salad and the dressing in separate containers. Put salad in pita half and top with dressing just before eating. Short-grain rice is the best choice for this recipe. It is stickier, which will help the salad hold together better. To vary, try apple chunks in place of mandarin oranges. Omit ginger in dressing, if you prefer. This recipe also makes a great main dish salad.

D O - A H E A D T I P S

Prepare rice up to a week ahead and refrigerate. The salad can be made the day before serving.

Salad:

2	Cups brown rice
$^1/_4$	Cup celery, thinly sliced
$^1/_4$	Cup scallions, sliced
$^1/_2$	Cup mandarin orange sections
$^1/_2$	Cup cucumber, sliced and seeded
$^1/_4$	Cup raisins
$^1/_4$	Cup pecans *or* walnuts (optional)

Dressing:

1	Cup nonfat plain yogurt *or* **Tofu Whipped Cream** (recipe in variation section)
2	Tablespoons orange juice
1	Tablespoon honey (optional)
$^1/_4$	Teaspoon ginger

❶ Cook the brown rice.

❷ In large bowl combine all salad items except rice. Toss warm rice into the salad ingredients.

❸ In small bowl, combine all dressing ingredients; mix well. Pour dressing over salad; toss gently to coat. Place salad in pita halves, *or* serve on bed of lettuce as a main dish salad.

PROTOSE PITA SANDWICHES

Serves 12

Preparation time: 15 minutes
Cooking time: 10 minutes

R E C I P E   T I P S

Protose,® a Worthington vegetarian product, is an excellent protein source, well-suited to sandwiches. It comes in a can and is available in some supermarkets and most health food stores. For a brown-bag lunch, place half a Protose patty in each pita and wrap tightly in plastic wrap. Put the dressing and the tomato slices in separate containers to be added just before eating.

D O - A H E A D   T I P S

Prepare Protose patties ahead of time and freeze if desired. Thaw patties in microwave. The dressing can be prepared 2-3 days ahead.

◆

Protose Patties:

1	20-ounce can Worthington Protose
$1/2$	Teaspoon garlic powder
2	Teaspoons ground cumin
1	Tablespoon coriander
2	Tablespoons sesame seeds

Dressing:

$1/2$	Cup plain nonfat yogurt
or $1/2$	Cup **Tofu Whipped Cream** (recipe in variation section)
$1/4$	Cup diced onion
1	Tablespoon coriander

Sandwich

6	Pita rounds, warmed, halved
12	Tomato slices
1	Cup alfalfa sprouts

❶ In food processor bowl, combine first 5 ingredients. Process until thoroughly mixed. Turn out of bowl and shape with hands into 6 patties.

❷ In small mixing bowl, prepare dressing by combining yogurt, onion, and coriander and mixing well.

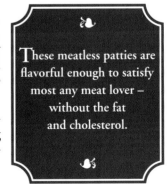

These meatless patties are flavorful enough to satisfy most any meat lover – without the fat and cholesterol.

❸ Heat small amount of oil over medium heat in nonstick skillet. Fry Protose patties until golden on each side. (For a lower-fat alternative, you can bake patties on a baking sheet sprayed with nonstick spray. Spray top of patties with nonstick spray and bake at 400° F for 8-10 minutes. Turn and continue baking until both sides are nicely browned.)

❹ Place half a patty inside each pita half and top with tomato, alfalfa sprouts, and yogurt dressing. Serve 2 pita sandwiches as a main course.

GOPHER SANDWICH

Serves 1

Preparation time: 5 minutes

R E C I P E   T I P S

This is a great lunch for kids to make themselves. Top the peanut butter layer with chopped apples, grated carrots, or raisins for a change.

◆

1	Pita bread half *or* flour tortilla
1 - 2	Tablespoons of peanut butter, creamy *or* chunky
1	Teaspoon honey
1	Teaspoon sunflower seeds

❶ Spread peanut butter in pita, covering both inside surfaces, or in a large circle to about one inch from outside edge of tortilla.

❷ Spread honey on top of the peanut butter and sprinkle with sunflower seeds. Pita is now ready to be eaten or wrapped. Roll the flour tortilla from one end to eat now or wrap tightly in plastic wrap for later.

Kids really "go-pher" this sandwich!

Part Two: The Home-Style Lunch

This section concentrates on some special sandwiches designed to be eaten at home–whatever the occasion–at a leisurely weekend cookout, for the perfect party luncheon, or when it's "just family." One or two have traveling possibilities and brown-bag tips are given. All are quick and easy–all are heart-healthy, and every single one is singularly delicious.

PECAN MEATBALL HOAGIE

Serves 5-6
Preparation time: 20 minutes
Baking time: 30 minutes

R E C I P E   T I P S
If you make the tofu version of this recipe, increase the garlic powder and sage to heaping teaspoons—tofu is bland and needs more seasoning. The meatballs with tomato sauce make a great entrée served over pasta. For a brown-bag version, take the meatballs and sauce in a separate container. Place in hoagie roll at lunchtime and enjoy!

D O - A H E A D   T I P S
Make a large batch of these meatballs and freeze loose in freezer bags until needed. Drop, frozen, into the tomato sauce and bake for 30 minutes, or warm in microwave on high for approximately 10 minutes.

◆

Pecan Meatballs

8	Ounces low-fat cottage cheese
8	Egg whites
or 2	Cups Morningstar Farms Better 'n Eggs®

Nondairy version, replace the first two ingredients with

16	Ounces of tofu, blended smooth
1	Large onion, chopped coarsely
1	Cup pecans, chopped coarsely
2	Cups Ritz *or* soda crackers, crushed coarsely
1	Teaspoon sage (1 ½ teaspoons sage in nondairy version)
2	Teaspoons garlic powder (3 teaspoons garlic powder in nondairy version)

Sandwich:

5	Whole-grain hoagie rolls
1 ½ - 2	Quarts tomato sauce
	Olive oil
2	Whole garlic cloves, peeled, *or* garlic powder

❶ In blender container, blend cottage cheese *or* tofu until smooth. Add a little water to the tofu if necessary to blend. Pour into mixing bowl. For dairy version, add the egg whites *or* Better 'n Eggs and mix thoroughly.

❷ Add the remaining ingredients and mix well.

❸ Allow to thicken in refrigerator for 10 minutes. Form mixture into 2-inch balls. Fry in lightly oiled pan, turning to brown on all sides. *Or,* lightly oil a baking sheet and bake meatballs at 400° F, turning several times, until all sides are browned. Be careful not to overcook and dry out meatballs in the oven. Start checking at 10 minutes and bake no longer than 30 minutes.

I adapted this low-fat, no-cholesterol version from Mom's original recipe, which was made with cream cheese and eggs. This one is just as good.

❹ Put browned meatballs in baking dish, cover with tomato sauce and heat in oven or microwave until sauce bubbles.

❺ Cut hoagie rolls in half and lightly brush cut sides with olive oil. If using fresh garlic, toast rolls in 400° F oven until lightly browned, remove from oven and rub garlic clove on each side. Bake an additional 3 to 4 minutes or until nicely browned.

❻ If using garlic powder, sprinkle each hoagie roll half lightly before toasting. Bake in a 400° F oven 3 to 4 minutes or until golden brown.

❼ Put 3 meatballs with sauce down the center of each toasted hoagie roll and serve warm.

GRILLED EGGPLANT SANDWICH WITH OVEN-CURED TOMATOES

Serves 4

Preparation time: 20 minutes
Cooking time, eggplant: 10 minutes
Cooking time, tomatoes: 2 hours

R E C I P E   T I P S

Oven-dried plum tomatoes add a gourmet touch to this grilled eggplant sandwich, but fresh tomatoes may also be used. Any fresh or dried herb, or even chopped scallions, may be added to the dressing.

D O - A H E A D   T I P S

Oven-cured tomatoes can be made several days ahead, layered between parchment paper, sealed in an airtight container, and refrigerated.

◆

Dressing:

1	Cup low-fat plain yogurt
or 1	Cup **Tofu Sour Cream** (recipe in variation section)
1	Teaspoon fresh lemon juice
$^1/_4$	Teaspoon garlic powder

Sandwich:

1	Medium eggplant, sliced into $^1/_4$-inch slices
4	**Oven-cured plum tomatoes** (see recipe in this section)
1	Teaspoon salt
1 $^1/_2$	Tablespoons olive oil
	Garlic powder to taste
4	Slices whole-grain toast *or* whole-wheat pita rounds
	Mint leaves for garnish

Dressing:

❶ In small bowl combine all the dressing ingredients; mix well.

Sandwich

❶ Place slices of eggplant in colander and sprinkle with salt. Rinse and drain well.

❷ Brush both sides of eggplant slices with oil and sprinkle lightly with salt and garlic powder. Sear in a skillet over medium-high heat until both sides are well browned and eggplant is soft, *or* grill over medium-hot coals for about 3 minutes on each side.

(The eggplant also can be dipped in egg whites *or* Better 'n Eggs®, breaded with seasoned breading meal, and cooked in olive oil until crispy on each side.)

❸ Brush one side of each slice of bread with olive oil and toast in 400° F oven for 5 minutes or until lightly browned; *or* place pita rounds on baking sheet and heat in a 250° F oven. (Cut off a small edge to open pita.)

❹ Divide eggplant slices among four pieces of toast *or* pita rounds. Top eggplant layer with oven-cured tomatoes, add dressing, and garnish with mint leaves.

OVEN-CURED TOMATOES

Makes 16 to 24 pieces

Preparation time: 10 minutes
Cooking time: 2 hours
Drying time: Overnight

R E C I P E   T I P S

These tomatoes can be added to sandwiches, salads, cooked vegetables, and pasta. They require only a few minutes of hands-on preparation, but need 12 hours to dry out in the oven. With a little planning ahead, you can have oven-cured tomatoes ready for last-minute meals.

D O - A H E A D   T I P S

The oven-cured tomatoes can be prepared several days ahead and kept in the refrigerator.

◆

8	Fresh beefsteak *or* 12 plum tomatoes
	Extra-virgin olive oil
1	Teaspoon salt
1	Teaspoon garlic powder
1	Teaspoon sugar
2	Teaspoons fresh thyme leaves, basil, *or* oregano

❶ Heat oven to 250° F. Trim ends off beefsteak tomatoes and cut each into 3 thick slices; cut plum tomatoes in half lengthwise. Arrange cut side up on a baking sheet lined with parchment.

❷ Brush tomatoes with olive oil. Sprinkle with salt, garlic powder, sugar, and fresh herb of choice.

❸ Place in oven. If you have a gas oven with a pilot light, turn off heat after 2 hours and leave overnight. If you have an electric oven, bake for 2 hours, then turn to "warm" setting and leave overnight. When done, the tomatoes should be somewhat wrinkled and shrunken but still quite juicy. Refrigerate in plastic container with parchment between layers of cured tomatoes.

These zesty dried tomatoes add the perfect taste to sandwiches, salads, and pasta dishes.

FALAFELS WITH TAHINI SAUCE

Serves 8-10
Preparation time: 20 minutes
Cooking time: 30 minutes

R E C I P E   T I P S
This typical Lebanese meal will definitely be worth the extra few minutes of preparation time.

D O - A H E A D   T I P S
Keep a supply of falafels in the freezer for last-minute lunches. Freeze in air-tight plastic bags. The tahini dressing will last up to a week in the refrigerator.

◆

Falafels:

3	Cups cooked *or* canned garbanzo beans
$^1/_4$	Cup liquid from garbanzo beans
$^1/_4$	Cup wheat germ
1	Small onion, finely chopped
2	Garlic cloves, minced
4	Tablespoons fresh parsley, chopped
$^1/_4$	Cup sesame seeds
$^1/_4$	Teaspoon dried basil
$^1/_4$	Teaspoon dried oregano
1	Teaspoon cumin
1	Teaspoon chili powder
$^1/_4$	Cup lemon juice
$^3/_4$	Cup cracker crumbs *or* wheat germ

Tahini Dressing:

(Makes 1 $^3/_4$ cups *or* 28 1-tablespoon servings)

1	Cup purchased tahini (sesame seed paste)
or 2	Cups sesame seeds, blended with $^1/_4$ cup olive oil till consistency of butter.
$^1/_2$	Cup water
$^1/_4$ - $^1/_2$	Cup plain yogurt

or

$^1/_4$ - $^1/_2$	Cup nondairy **Tofu Sour Cream** (recipe in variation section)
2	Tablespoons lemon juice
3	Cloves fresh garlic, minced or crushed

Sandwich:

1	Whole-wheat pita half
2 - 3	Falafels
$^1/_4$ - $^1/_2$	Cup shredded lettuce

or

$^1/_4$ - $^1/_3$	Cup alfalfa sprouts
2	Tablespoons tomatoes, chopped
1	Teaspoon green onions, sliced
1	Tablespoon carrots, peeled and grated
1 - 2	Tablespoons Tahini Dressing

Falafels:

❶ In blender container, combine garbanzo beans and liquid and puree until smooth.

❷ Transfer bean mixture to a large bowl and add all other ingredients except cracker crumbs *or* wheat germ. Mix well.

Pungent herbs, earthy garlic and garbanzo beans, tangy tahini—who says healthful food has to be bland?

❸ Stir in enough cracker crumbs *or* wheat germ so the mixture will hold together.

❹ Roll mixture into 1$^1/_2$-inch balls. Place on a cookie sheet and bake in a preheated oven at 350° F for 10-15 minutes per side *or* until lightly browned with a crispy, dry, cracked exterior. Be careful not to let the falafels dry out too much. The inside should be moist.

Tahini Dressing:

❶ In blender container, combine all dressing ingredients and blend until smooth. Refrigerate until serving time.

To assemble:

❶ Open up pita half and fill with 2 crushed falafels. Drizzle with $^1/_2$ tablespoon of Tahini Dressing. Top with lettuce *or* sprouts, tomatoes, green onions, and shredded carrots. Drizzle with an additional $^1/_2$ tablespoon of Tahini Dressing. Serve.

CIRCULAR SUBMARINE SANDWICH

Serves 10-12
Preparation time: 20 minutes
Cooking time: 15 minutes

R E C I P E   T I P S
The ingredients for this oversized sub can be varied to suit your taste. Add tomatoes, grated carrots, and any variety of fresh or dried herbs. The Worthington luncheon meats are a must in this sandwich. These delicious meat substitutes come presliced and frozen, and may be purchased in natural food stores or some supermarkets.

D O - A H E A D   T I P S
The peppers can be roasted and prepared several days ahead and refrigerated, or to save time, you can purchase roasted red peppers in a jar.

◆

1	Red bell pepper
1	Yellow pepper
1	Eggplant
1	Large onion, sliced in thin circles
	Olive oil
	Salt to taste (optional)
1	10-inch round loaf whole-grain bread
$^1/_2$	Cup Oregano-Lemon Vinaigrette (recipe follows)
10	Slices of Worthington Vegetarian "Corned Beef," "Smoked Turkey," etc.
10	Tomato slices, $^1/_2$-inch thick
20	Fresh basil leaves (*or* spinach leaves sprinkled with dried basil)

❶ Roast peppers under broiler or, using tongs, hold over a gas flame until completely blackened. Place peppers in a paper bag until cool. Peel and seed. Cut in half and set aside.

❷ Slice eggplant into $^5/_8$-inch-thick slices. Lightly brush with oil and cook on a grill or in a hot skillet until brown on both sides. Season with salt and garlic powder. In same skillet lightly brown onion circles in small amount of water *or* olive oil.

❸ Cut bread in half horizontally; scoop out some of the inside of the top half. Brush bottom half with $^1/_4$ cup vinaigrette. Layer the sandwich in this order: overlapped luncheon meat slices (alternating flavors if desired), tomato slices, eggplant, onion circles, and roasted peppers. Top with fresh basil leaves *or* spinach leaves sprinkled with basil. Brush inside of top half of bread with remaining vinaigrette and place on sandwich. Cut into wedges and serve.

OREGANO-LEMON VINAIGRETTE

Makes 1 cup

$^1/_4$	Cup fresh lemon juice
2	Small bunches fresh oregano (about $^1/_2$ cup)
$^3/_4$	Cup extra-virgin olive oil
2	Whole garlic cloves
2	Tablespoons capers, drained and rinsed
	Salt to taste (optional)

❶ In blender container, combine all ingredients. Blend until smooth.

Pictured on page 30

This sub is a winner. It's gourmet, it's meatless and healthful, and it's scrumptious!

Part Three: Soup for Lunch

Each of these easy-to-make soups is a one-dish-meal that can be served hot or cold. The other possibilities are endless. Soup can be served as an appetizer before a hearty dinner, or popped into a thermos as part of a brown-bag lunch. Its the perfect on-the-go meal. Just add a whole-grain bread and some fresh vegetables and you have a wonderful lunch or light supper.

MINESTRONE SOUP

Serves 8

Preparation time: 20 minutes
Cooking time: 1 hour and 20 minutes

RECIPE TIPS

Use canned beans to speed up preparation. You can use frozen vegetables, but I think the fresh ones are worth the few extra minutes. Vary the vegetables to suit your taste.

DO-AHEAD TIPS

Cook the dried beans a day or two ahead, if you like. This soup tastes even better after 2 to 3 days. Make a large batch for Sunday lunch, then take some to work in a thermos on Monday or Tuesday. Crunchy hard bread or warm homemade bread makes a great accompaniment to this meal.

◆

¹/₂		Cup dried kidney *or* garbanzo beans
or	4	Cups canned kidney *or* garbanzo beans
	2	Tablespoons olive oil
	1	Large onion, chopped
	3	Stalks of celery, sliced
	2	Cloves garlic, finely chopped *or* pressed
	4	Cups water
	4	Teaspoons McKay's Chicken-Style Seasoning
	2	Teaspoons dried basil
or	2	Tablespoons fresh basil leaves, crumbled
	1	Quart canned tomatoes, broken up
	1	6-ounce can tomato paste
¹/₂		Cup shell macaroni (uncooked)
	2	Medium carrots, pared and sliced
	2	Medium zucchini, chopped (about 2 cups)
	1	Cup fresh *or* frozen spinach, chopped (optional)

❶ Preparation of dried beans: Cover dried beans with water in large saucepan. Refrigerate overnight. Or to quick-soak beans, bring to a boil in water over high heat; cook 2 minutes. Remove from heat and let stand 1 hour. Drain beans.

❷ In large saucepan, heat oil over medium heat. Add onion and celery. Sauté, stirring occasionally, for 8 to 10 minutes or until tender. Add garlic and sauté, stirring occasionally, for 2 more minutes.

❸ Add water, McKay's Chicken-Style Seasoning, prepared dried *or* canned beans, and basil. Bring to a boil over high heat. Lower heat; cover and simmer 1 hour. Add tomatoes, tomato paste, and dry pasta. Return to boil. (Add more water at this point if you like a more brothy soup.) Lower heat; cover and simmer 5 to 7 minutes or until pasta is partially cooked. Add carrots; simmer for 5 more minutes. Add zucchini and spinach and simmer for an additional 5 minutes or until carrots and zucchini are crisp-tender. Do not overcook vegetables. Serve.

My friend Sue Neibauer frequently makes this Italian specialty for Family Night at our church.

VEGETABLE SOUP

Serves 10-12
Preparation time: 15 minutes
Cooking time: 30-40 minutes

M E N U   T I P S
Try topping this soup with dumplings for a change of pace. Just drop about 10 spoonfuls of dumpling or biscuit dough on top of nearly done soup, cover tightly and simmer for 12 to 15 minutes. Don't be afraid of the peanut butter in this recipe. It adds a wonderful creamy richness to the soup. Brown-baggers, this soup travels well in a thermos. Homemade bread is the best accompaniment.

D O - A H E A D   T I P S
This recipe can be made several days before serving and refrigerated in an airtight container. It cannot be frozen because potatoes get mushy and fall apart when frozen.

◆

10	Cups water
2	Cups potatoes, cut in large chunks
1	Cup carrots, pared and sliced
1	Cup celery, sliced
1	Large onion, chopped
2	Cups fresh **or** frozen lima beans
2	Cups fresh **or** frozen green peas
2	Cups fresh **or** frozen green beans
2	Cups fresh **or** frozen corn
2	Cups canned whole tomatoes, crushed
1/2	Cup peanut butter
4	Tablespoons margarine (optional)
2	Cloves garlic, minced
1	Tablespoon dried basil
1	Tablespoon dried oregano
1	Tablespoon dried thyme
1	Tablespoon dried parsley
1	Tablespoon brown sugar (optional)
2	Packets Onion **or** Golden-flavored G. Washington Broth mix
1	Tablespoon McKay's Chicken-Style Seasoning

> **M**y friend Jacquelyn Cromwell serves this delicious Vegetable Soup topped with dumplings.

1	Cup cabbage, shredded
1	Cup zucchini, halved and sliced
1/2	Cup mushrooms, sliced (optional)

❶ In large Dutch oven or pot, simmer first nine ingredients until potatoes are done.

❷ In blender container, combine tomatoes, peanut butter, margarine, garlic, dried herbs, sugar, G. Washington Broth mix and McKay's Chicken-Style Seasoning. Blend just a few seconds until peanut butter is mixed thoroughly and tomatoes are in small chunks.

❸ Add blender mixture to simmering vegetables. Add cabbage, zucchini, and mushrooms and cook an additional 10 minutes.

CHILLED CUCUMBER-SPINACH SOUP

Serves 4-6
Preparation time: 10 minutes
Cooking time: 5 minutes

R E C I P E   T I P S
Serve this refreshing soup as a delicious appetizer to a summer meal.

◆

10 - 12	Ounces chopped fresh spinach, steamed until wilted
2	Cups nonfat milk **or** tofu milk
2	Cups plain yogurt **or** **Tofu Sour Cream** (recipe in variation section)
1	Large cucumber, finely chopped
	Juice from 1/2 lemon
3	Tablespoons fresh dill, minced,
or 3	Teaspoons dry dill leaves
1	Teaspoon curry powder

❶ Combine all ingredients, mixing thoroughly. Chill well before serving.

This light-tasting cold soup recipe comes from Jacquelyn Cromwell's large repertoire of great soup recipes.

MILLET MUSHROOM SOUP

Serves 10
Preparation time: 15 minutes
Cooking time: 30 - 35 minutes

R E C I P E   T I P S
This recipe is perfect kept warm in a thermos for a fall picnic or a brown-bag lunch. Add multigrain bread and some fresh vegetable sticks for a delicious, well-balanced meal.

◆

1	Cup hulled millet
2	Quarts water
2	Cups canned whole tomatoes
1 ¹/₂	Cups tomato puree
2	Garlic cloves, minced
1	Tablespoon fresh *or* 1 teaspoon dried basil
1 - 2	Packages Onion *or* Golden flavored G. Washington Broth mix, to taste
1	Green pepper, chopped
1	Large onion, chopped coarsely
1	Cup celery, chopped
1	Cup fresh mushrooms, thickly sliced

❶ In large pan bring 2 quarts of water to a boil; add millet and cook for 20 minutes.

❷ In blender or food processor, combine canned whole tomatoes, tomato puree, garlic, basil, and contents of broth packets. Blend a few seconds until whole tomatoes are in small pieces. Add tomato mixture to the millet and let simmer.

❸ Add onion and pepper to the simmering soup and cook until vegetables are just soft.

❹ Add fresh mushrooms. Continue cooking only until mushrooms are just heated through. Serve.

Mushrooms, tomatoes, and a tasty broth added to millet make a delicious combination.

I never liked soup as a child. I didn't care for it much as a grown-up, either, until Deidre Jepson shared this easy-to-make, low-fat soup recipe with me.

CORN CHOWDER

Serves 6
Preparation time: 10 minutes
Cooking time: 20-30 minutes

R E C I P E   T I P S
Be sure to try the nondairy version of this recipe. It tastes just as good as the dairy version. Brown-baggers, this one keeps well in a thermos.

D O - A H E A D   T I P S
Cashew-Rice Cream can be made up to a week ahead of time and stored in an airtight container in the refrigerator.

◆

4	Cups potatoes, cut in large chunks
1	Large onion, chopped coarsely
1	Large green pepper, chopped
2	Cups fresh *or* frozen corn
1	Cup low-fat evaporated milk
or 1	Cup **Cashew-Rice Cream** (see recipe in variation section)

❶ In large soup pan, cook potatoes, onion, and green pepper, in just enough water to cover the tops of the vegetable mixture. Bring to a boil; turn temperature down and simmer for 10 minutes.

❷ Add corn and simmer for an additional 10 minutes, or until vegetables are softened. Add milk of your choice. Allow soup to return to a boil; remove from heat and serve. (If using Cashew-Rice Cream, allow soup to simmer for 5 to 10 minutes after cream has been added.) Serve warm.

CREAM OF BROCCOLI SOUP

Serves 8
Preparation time: 20 minutes
Cooking time: 25 minutes

RECIPE TIPS

This soup has a wonderful creamy texture, whether it's made with or without dairy products. If you prefer bite-sized broccoli florets, add them at the end of the recipe. Try substituting cauliflower or a blend of other vegetables for the broccoli. This soup keeps well in a thermos.

DO-AHEAD TIPS

The Cashew-Rice Cream can be prepared up to a week in advance. The finished soup can be kept in the refrigerator for up to a week.

◆

2	Cups water
1 $\frac{1}{2}$	Pounds fresh **or** frozen broccoli florets
1	Large stalk celery, chopped (about $\frac{3}{4}$ cup)
1	Medium onion, chopped (about $\frac{1}{2}$ cup)
2	Tablespoons margarine
2	Tablespoons flour
2 $\frac{1}{2}$	Cups water
1	Tablespoon McKay's Chicken-Style Seasoning
1	Teaspoon garlic powder
	Salt to taste (optional)
1	Cup low-fat evaporated milk
or 1	Cup **Cashew-Rice Cream** (recipe in variation section)

❶ In 3-quart saucepan combine 2 cups water, broccoli, celery, and onion. Cover and heat to boiling. Cook just until tender, about 10 minutes; do not drain.

❷ Working in batches if necessary, transfer mixture to food processor or blender. Blend to uniform consistency.

❸ To make white sauce: melt margarine in 3-quart saucepan over low heat. Stir in flour. Cook, stirring constantly, until mixture is smooth and bubbly; remove from heat. Stir in 2 $\frac{1}{2}$ cups water. Heat to boiling, stirring constantly. Boil and stir 1 minute.

❹ Add to white sauce: broccoli mixture, McKay's Chicken-Style seasoning, garlic powder, and salt. (For a chunky variation, you can add 2 cups of small broccoli florets at this point and boil about 5 minutes or until crisp-tender.

Other vegetables can also be added.) Bring to boil. Add milk of your choice. (If using evaporated milk, cook only until heated through; do not boil the milk. The Cashew-Rice Cream, however, tastes best if it simmers with the soup at least 5 minutes.)

A flavorful, fix-it-fast, low-fat, guilt-free version of an old favorite.

TOMATO CORN CHOWDER

Serves 15   Makes 5 quarts
Preparation time: 15 minutes
Cooking time: 25 minutes

MENU TIPS

Add whole-grain rolls and fresh vegetable sticks for a complete balanced meal. Loma Linda Big Franks, a vegetarian version of Polish sausage, add a spicy full-bodied flavor to this one-dish meal. They come in a can and can be bought at health food stores and some larger supermarket chains.

DO-AHEAD TIPS

This soup can be made ahead and stored for several days in the refrigerator.

◆

1	Large onion, chopped coarsely
1	20-ounce can Loma Linda Big Franks®, sliced
2	Quarts tomatoes, pureed
3	Potatoes, diced
3	Cups hot water
2	Cups fresh **or** frozen corn
$\frac{1}{2}$	Teaspoon paprika
1	Tablespoon sugar
	Salt to taste
12	Ounces nonfat evaporated milk
2	Cups **Cashew-Rice Cream** (recipe in variation section) **or** soy milk

❶ In 8-quart saucepan, sauté onion and sliced Loma Linda Big Franks until browned.

❷ Add remaining ingredients. Bring to boil and cook until tender.

❸ Add milk of your choice; heat through and serve.

This recipe comes from my friend Wendy's big country kitchen. Homemade soup and bread are a much-loved Friday night tradition at her home.

Soup for Lunch

This "meaty" vegetarian stew is perfect served with crusty French bread.

"BEEF" VEGETABLE STEW

Serves 8
Preparation time: 15 minutes
Cooking time: 30 minutes

RECIPE TIPS

This vegetarian stew features a wheat-based meat substitute called Worthington Vegetable Steaks. This product comes in a can and can be purchased at most natural food stores and some larger supermarkets. To make a "chicken" version, replace the soy sauce with 2 tablespoons of McKay's Chicken-Style seasoning and use Golden or Onion G. Washington Broth mix rather than the Beefy Brown flavor. Replace the Vegetable Steaks with Loma Linda Tender Bits, another good canned meat substitute, or tofu. Make a wonderful potpie by placing the finished stew in a baking dish, covering it with a pastry dough crust, and baking at 400° F for 30-40 minutes or until crust is golden brown and stew is bubbling. This stew keeps well in a thermos.

DO-AHEAD TIPS

This recipe tastes best if it stands several hours before serving. It can be made in a Crock Pot and simmered on low heat while you're at work.

◆

4	Raw potatoes, cubed
4	Carrots, sliced
2	Stalks celery, sliced thin
1 - 2	Packets G. Washington Broth mix, Dark Brown, to taste
2	Tablespoons canola oil *or* water
1	Large onion, chopped coarsely
1	20-ounce can Worthington Vegetable Steaks, cut in strips *or* cubed
3	Tablespoons all-purpose flour
1	Cup water
1	Teaspoon garlic powder
3	Tablespoons light soy sauce
2	Teaspoons Vegex seasoning paste (optional)
1	Cup frozen green peas *or* green beans

❶ In 8-quart saucepan, cook potatoes, carrots, and celery in enough water to just cover all the vegetables. Stir in the G. Washington Broth mix. Cook until just tender. (Do not drain.)

❷ Sauté onions and vegetable steaks in oil *or* water until lightly browned. Sprinkle with flour. Mix together 1 cup water, garlic powder, soy sauce, and Savorex. Pour over steaks and onions. Stir until the flour is dissolved.

❸ Add this mixture to the cooked vegetables in large saucepan. Add peas *or* green beans and simmer until stew is thickened. Add additional soy sauce *or* broth mix to desired taste. Serve hot.

This mouthwatering, robust stew is one of my husband's favorites.

SPINACH TOFU SOUP

Serves 10
Preparation time: 10 minutes
Cooking time: 40 minutes
Makes 6 quarts

MENU TIPS

This Oriental-style broth-based soup is a perfect appetizer before a full-course meal. It also stands well alone as a light lunch served with a sandwich and some crisp fresh vegetables on the side.

◆

12	Cups water
1 1/2	Cups brown rice
8	Packets of G. Washington Broth mix, Golden, Onion, *or* Rich Brown flavors
1	Large onion, chopped
5	Garlic cloves, minced *or* chopped
1	Pound firm tofu, cut in 1/2-inch cubes
10	Ounces fresh spinach leaves, chopped
	Garlic salt to taste

❶ In 8 quart-saucepan, combine water, rice, broth mix, onion, and garlic. Bring to a boil and let simmer for 20 minutes.

❷ Add tofu cubes to simmering broth mixture, and cook an additional 15 minutes.

❸ Add fresh chopped spinach leaves and cook an additional 5 minutes. Serve with garlic salt available for individual servings.

"CHICKEN" NOODLE SOUP

Serves 8-10
Preparation time: 10 minutes
Cooking time: 35 minutes

RECIPE TIPS

This recipe features a vegetarian substitute for chicken, Worthington FriChik®, which adds a flavor and texture much like real chicken. Serve this traditional soup with whole-grain bread and a green salad for a perfect lunch or light dinner. Brown-baggers, this soup travels well in a thermos.

◆

8	Cups water
6	Potatoes, diced
1	Large onion, chopped coarsely
3 - 4	Carrots, sliced thin
1	12.5-ounce can Worthington FriChik, chopped
2	Tablespoons McKay's Chicken-Style Seasoning
1	Teaspoon garlic powder
2	Tablespoons fresh *or* 2 teaspoons dried parsley
2	Bay leaves
	Salt to taste
2	Cups egg noodles, uncooked
1	Cup frozen peas
1	Cup skimmed evaporated milk *or* tofu milk

❶ In an 8-quart saucepan, combine water, potatoes, onions, carrots and bring to boil. Simmer for 15 minutes or until tender. Add FriChik and seasonings.

❷ Add noodles and peas to simmering vegetables and cook an additional 10 minutes.

❸ Add milk and heat thoroughly and serve.

This soup was my mom's favorite comfort food whenever her children were sick.

BORSCHT

Serves 10
Preparation time: 10 minutes
Cooking time: 30 minutes

M E N U   T I P S

This hearty soup makes a whole meal of delicious root vegetables. Crusty hard bread and crunchy fresh vegetables complete the meal.

◆

2	Quarts water
1	Quart canned tomatoes, crushed
2	Packets G. Washington Broth mix, Dark Brown flavor
3	Potatoes, diced
2	Large carrots, sliced
2	Stalks celery, sliced
1	Large onion, chopped coarsely
3	Teaspoons fresh lemon juice
2	Teaspoons dill seed
$^1/_2$	Medium head cabbage, shredded
3 - 4	Medium-sized fresh beets, peeled and diced
4	Tablespoons margarine (optional)
	Salt to taste

❶ In 8-quart saucepan, combine all ingredients and cook until tender. The beets will be just crisp tender.

❷ Serve, if desired, with a dollop of low-fat sour cream *or* Tofu Sour Cream (recipe in variation section) on each individual serving.

Here's a good way to get your family to try a dish containing beets.

Hot sauce adds a zesty punch to this gourmet tomato soup.

HERB TOMATO SOUP

Serves 8   Makes 3 quarts
Preparation time: 10 minutes
Cooking time: 30 minutes

M E N U   T I P S

Serve this soup with crackers and a tossed green salad for a nutritious, light lunch or as the perfect appetizer for a gourmet dinner! This soup can be made up to a week ahead and stored in the refrigerator.

◆

1	Medium onion, chopped
2	Tablespoons margarine
4	Cups water
1	Quart canned whole tomatoes, crushed
2	Medium carrots, sliced
2	Stalks celery, sliced
1	Teaspoon sugar
1	Tablespoon McKay's Chicken-Style Seasoning
1	Tablespoon fresh *or* 1 teaspoon dried basil leaves
$^1/_2$	Teaspoon dried thyme
$^1/_4$	Teaspoon dried savory (optional)
$^1/_8$	Teaspoon ground mace
	Salt to taste
2	Tablespoons hot sauce, optional

❶ In 6-quart saucepan, combine all ingredients and bring to a boil. Reduce heat and simmer about 30 minutes or until vegetables are tender. Serve hot.

Part Four: Salad for Lunch

Salads have always been the healthful side dish in a multicourse meal, but more and more, they have come into their own as main courses. With all our health concerns today, salads make us feel that we are being good to our bodies. And they offer abundant combinations of intriguing flavors, textures, and colors. If you're tired of your mundane repertoire of meals, perk up your life and go with the greens!

HERBED PASTA SALAD

Serves 6-8   Makes 7-8 cups
Preparation time: 15 minutes
Cooking time: 10 minutes

R E C I P E   T I P S

Try making this pasta salad with a variety of fresh vegetables. Different pasta shapes and flavors can also be used. A commercial Italian dressing can replace this homemade version. Just check the label for fat content. Tofu Ranch Dressing (recipe in the dressing section) would also taste good in place of the oil-based dressing.

D O - A H E A D   T I P S

The pasta noodles can be cooked ahead of time and stored in an airtight plastic bag. The pasta salad tastes best if made up several hours ahead and chilled until serving time, but be sure to leave the tomato and avocado slices out until just before serving.

◆

Salad:

$^3/_4$	Cup spiral noodles, uncooked
1	Cup broccoli florets
1	Cup cauliflower florets
$^1/_2$	Cup carrots, sliced *or* shredded
$^1/_2$	Cup red pepper, chopped
1	4-ounce jar water-packed artichoke hearts, drained and chopped (may also use marinated)
$^1/_2$	Cup pitted black olives, whole *or* sliced
$^1/_4$	Cup green onions, sliced thinly
$^1/_2$	Medium avocado, sliced
1	Medium tomato, chopped
$^1/_2$	Cup Italian Salad Dressing

Italian Salad Dressing:

$^1/_3$	Cup canola vegetable oil
4	Tablespoons fresh lemon juice
1	Garlic clove, minced *or* pressed through garlic press
1	Tablespoon fresh parsley
1	Tablespoon fresh *or* 1 teaspoon dried basil leaves
1	Tablespoon fresh *or* 1 teaspoon dried oregano leaves
$^1/_2$	Teaspoon salt

❶ Cook pasta in boiling water for approximately 10 minutes or until just tender. Do not overcook. Pour cooked pasta into colander and rinse with cold water; drain well.

❷ In large mixing bowl, combine pasta, broccoli, cauliflower, carrots, red pepper, artichoke hearts, black olives, and green onions. Toss well.

❸ Prepare Italian Dressing. Pour over pasta and vegetable mixture; toss well and chill for several hours.

❹ Just before serving, add avocado slices and tomato wedges, reserving a few slices of each to garnish individual servings or salad bowl.

My daughter, Cherié, loves this hearty pasta salad. It adds flair and nutrients to any meal.

CITRUS RICE SALAD

Serves 5   Makes 5 cups
Preparation time: 15 minutes
Cooking time (for rice): 35 minutes

R E C I P E   T I P S

This salad combines grains, fruits, vegetables, and nuts, tossed in a light and creamy dressing. One serving gives you all the protein and carbohydrates you need for a balanced meal. Serve on a bed of lettuce of your choice.

D O - A H E A D   T I P S

The rice can be prepared ahead of time. If you use Tofu Whipped Cream topping, it can be made several days ahead of time and stored in the refrigerator in a sealed container.

◆

Salad:

2	Cups brown rice, cooked
$^1/_4$	Cup celery, thinly sliced
$^1/_4$	Cup scallions, sliced
$^1/_2$	Cup mandarin oranges
$^1/_2$	Cup cucumber, sliced and seeded
$^1/_4$	Cup raisins
$^1/_4$	Cup pecans *or* walnuts (optional)

Dressing:

1	Cup nonfat plain yogurt *or* **Tofu Whipped Cream** (recipe in variation section)
2	Tablespoons orange juice
2	Tablespoons honey *or* sugar
$^1/_4$	Teaspoon ginger

❶ Cook the brown rice.

❷ In large bowl, combine all salad items except rice and mix well. Then toss warm rice into the salad ingredients.

❸ In small bowl, combine all dressing ingredients; mix well. Pour dressing over salad; toss gently to coat. Serve a hearty portion of this salad on a bed of dark green lettuce as a main dish.

TACO SALAD

Serves 8-10
Preparation time: 15 minutes

R E C I P E   T I P S

This main-dish salad is great garnished with whole tortilla chips. The beans and the tofu from the nondairy option give the necessary protein, the tortilla chips provide the grain, and the remaining ingredients provide the vegetables—a balanced meal all in one dish.

D O - A H E A D   T I P S

The salad ingredients—except the chips, dressing, and tomatoes—can be tossed together the day before serving. The dressing can be made the day before serving and chilled.

◆

Salad:

1	Head iceberg *or* green leaf lettuce, torn into bite-sized pieces
1	Can kidney beans
3 - 4	Medium tomatoes, chopped
$^3/_4$	Cup sliced olives
7-	Ounce can green chili peppers, chopped
6 - 8	Cups low-salt tortilla chips, broken in large pieces

Taco Salad Dressing:

1	Avocado, pitted and peeled
2	Tablespoons taco sauce, hot *or* mild to your taste
$^1/_2$	Cup low-fat sour cream
or $^1/_2$	Cup **Tofu Sour Cream** (recipe in variation section)
$^3/_4$	Teaspoon chili powder
$^1/_2$	Teaspoon cumin
$^1/_4$	Teaspoon salt (optional)
3	Tablespoons minced onion

❶ In large mixing bowl, combine all salad ingredients except tortilla chips, and toss together.

❷ In food processor, process with chop blade all ingredients for dressing until smooth. For nondairy version, combine in food processor all ingredients for **Tofu Sour Cream** with all the dressing ingredients (except the sour cream) and process together until smooth.

❸ Just before serving, toss chips and dressing into salad mixture. Serve immediately.

My sister-in-law, Jolene, is a taco salad expert. This recipe is one of her favorites.

SPINACH SALAD SUPREME

Serves 8-10
Preparation time: 15 minutes

R E C I P E   T I P S
A sweet dressing adds the perfect touch to this colorful salad. Try sprinkling with sesame seeds or sunflower seeds for variety.

D O - A H E A D   T I P S
The Honey Salad Dressing can be made several days ahead and stored in the refrigerator until serving time.

◆

Salad:

1 $^1/_2$	Pounds fresh spinach leaves, torn into bite-sized pieces
1	Cup alfalfa *or* bean sprouts
1	Small onion, sliced in thin circles *or* 4-5 scallions, sliced thin
1	Can mandarin oranges, drained
$^3/_4$	Cup fresh mushrooms, sliced
1	8-ounce can water chestnuts, diced
$^1/_2$-$^3/_4$	Cup toasted almonds, sliced

Honey Salad Dressing:

$^1/_4$	Cup lemon juice
$^3/_4$	Cup canola oil
$^1/_4$	Teaspoon paprika
$^1/_2$	Teaspoon salt (optional)
1	Teaspoon sugar
$^1/_2$	Cup honey

❶ In jar with tight-fitting lid, combine all the salad dressing ingredients. Shake well and chill.

❷ In large salad bowl, combine all salad ingredients except almonds, and toss well.

❸ Just before serving, shake dressing and pour over salad. Toss well, coating evenly, and garnish with almonds.

This salad is a favorite recipe from my friend Doris Pierce.

CHEF'S SALAD

Serves 1
Preparation time: 10 minutes

R E C I P E   T I P S
A wide variety of vegetables can be used in this recipe. Vegetarian meat substitutes, such as Worthington Smoked Turkey will add an extra taste treat.

◆

Salad:

2	Cups lettuce leaves (use a variety, if possible, such as green leaf, romaine, and Boston lettuce)
$^1/_4$	Cup carrots, shredded
$^1/_4$	Cup canned garbanzo beans
1	Small tomato, cut into wedges
$^1/_2$	Avocado, peeled, pitted, and sliced in wedges
$^1/_2$	Small sweet onion, sliced and separated into rings
$^1/_4$	Cup seasoned croutons
4	Black *or* green pitted olives, halved
	Salad dressing of choice

❶ On large dinner plate layer a variety of lettuce leaves torn into bite-sized pieces. Arrange on top of lettuce layer carrots and garbanzo beans.

❷ Garnish salad with tomato wedges, avocado wedges, onion circles, croutons, and olives. Top with salad dressing of choice. Try the Nondairy Ranch Dressing *or* the Italian Herb Dressing from the dressing recipes.

Choose the youngest and freshest greens from your supermarket's produce section.

HERBED GARDEN SALAD

Serves 1
Preparation time: 5-10 minutes

RECIPE TIPS

Arrange this salad just before serving. Use any combination of greens you like. Choose some of the darker-green ones. Remember that the darker the green color, the more vitamin A (beta carotene) the salad greens contain.

◆

1 - 2	Cups of green *or* red leaf lettuce
$^1/_2$	Green onion with top, sliced thin
1	Small carrot, grated
$^1/_2$	Cucumber, sliced
1	Small tomato, cut in wedges
$^1/_4$	Cup alfalfa sprouts
	Fresh *or* dried herbs (basil, oregano, etc.) to taste
	Garlic powder to taste
1	Tablespoon sliced almonds (try toasting the almonds for a different taste)
	Salad dressing of choice

❶ On small salad plate, layer lettuce leaves torn into bite-sized pieces, green onions, and carrots.

❷ Arrange cucumbers, tomato wedges, and alfalfa sprouts on top. Sprinkle with fresh *or* dried herbs, garlic powder, and almonds. Drizzle dressing over all.

This is my son Kent's very favorite salad. He likes it served on an extra large plate, topped with Italian Herb Dressing.

FRUIT SLAW

Serves 4
Preparation time: 10 minutes
Marinating time: 4 - 24 hours

RECIPE TIPS

When you're pressed for time, open a bag of shredded cabbage and toss together this easy-to-prepare Fruit Slaw.

DO-AHEAD TIPS

Although this salad takes very little time to make, it does need plenty of time to marinate. Make sure you allow at least 4 hours.

◆

1	8-ounce can pineapple chunks (juice-packed)
2	Cups cabbage, shredded
$^2/_3$	Cup apple, chopped
$^1/_2$	Cup carrots, shredded
$^1/_4$	Cup green pepper, chopped
1	Tablespoon vegetable oil
1	Tablespoon honey
1	Tablespoon lemon juice
$^1/_8$	Teaspoon ground ginger

❶ Drain pineapple chunks, reserving 2 tablespoons juice.

❷ In a large salad bowl, combine pineapple, cabbage, apple, carrots, and green pepper.

❸ Dressing: In a screw-top jar, combine reserved pineapple juice, oil, honey, lemon juice, ginger, and $^1/_8$ teaspoon salt. Cover and shake well.

❹ Pour dressing over salad. Toss lightly to coat evenly. Chill 4 to 24 hours. Toss again before serving. Serve with a slotted spoon to drain off excess dressing.

54

RASPBERRY-ASPARAGUS SPINACH SALAD

Serves 6
Preparation time: 20 minutes
Cooking time: 10 minutes

M E N U   T I P S

Serve this salad as a light lunch with hot whole-grain rolls. It features Worthington FriChik, a meatless chicken substitute, which comes in a can and can be purchased at most natural food stores and some larger supermarkets.

D O - A H E A D   T I P S

The asparagus and FriChik can be prepared several hours in advance and refrigerated. The dressing can be made ahead and kept in the refrigerator. (Stir the dressing well just before adding to salad.) The spinach leaves can be washed, torn, and chilled in sealed plastic bags a day ahead.

◆

Salad:

1 - 2	Tablespoons vegetable oil *or* water
2	12.5-ounce cans Worthington FriChik®, cut in long thin strips
18	Spears fresh asparagus, cut in 2-inch pieces (reserve a few long spears for garnish if desired)
1-Lb.	Bag fresh spinach leaves, washed and torn into bite-sized pieces
1	Bunch large spinach leaves, left whole
2	Peaches *or* nectarines, peeled and sliced
$^1/_2$	Cup fresh raspberries

Dressing:

1	Cup fresh *or* thawed frozen raspberries
3	Tablespoons lime *or* lemon juice
2	Tablespoons sugar *or* honey
$^1/_2$	Teaspoon salt
$^1/_2$	Cup vegetable oil

❶ Heat $^1/_2$ to 1 tablespoon of oil in large skillet over medium heat and add FriChik strips. Cook, turning to lightly brown all sides. Remove from the skillet and chill.

❷ Add remaining $^1/_2$ to 1 tablespoon of oil to the same skillet and add the cut asparagus, stirring over medium high heat for 2 to 3 minutes or until crisp-tender. If you are using water in place of fat, simply steam the asparagus, covered, about 3 minutes or until crisp-tender. Remove from skillet and chill. (To thoroughly chill asparagus and FriChik in the refrigerator takes an hour or two. To quick-chill for last-minute preparation, put asparagus and FriChik on individual plates and place in the freezer.)

❸ In blender or food processor with chop blade, combine all dressing ingredients except oil, blend till smooth. Continue to blend while slowly pouring in oil. Mixture will get frothy and thicken slightly. Cover and refrigerate.

❹ Just before serving, arrange large spinach leaves on 6 individual serving plates. Top each serving with sautéed FriChik strips, asparagus, and peach or nectarine slices. Drizzle with dressing and garnish with raspberries.

Salad for Lunch

TABOULI SALAD

Serves 10-12
Preparation time: 10 minutes
Marinating time: 2 hours

M E N U   T I P S
Bulgar wheat absorbs the flavor of the onions and other seasonings to create a great tasting salad, delicious with Mazidra (recipe in the dinner section) and pita bread—a perfect Middle Eastern dinner. For a light luncheon serve with Hummus Dip (recipe in the salad dressing section) and pita bread.

D O - A H E A D   T I P S
This recipe must marinate for a minimum of 2 hours before it is served. It can be made the day before if you add the lettuce and tomatoes just before serving.

◆

2	Medium onions, chopped
1	Teaspoon salt
	Juice of 2 limes
4	Tablespoons olive oil
2	Teaspoons dried mint, chopped,
or $^{1}/_{4}$	Cup fresh mint, chopped
1 $^{1}/_{2}$	Cups bulgar wheat
5	Large tomatoes, diced small
1	Large green *or* red pepper, diced small
2	Large cucumbers, diced small
$^{1}/_{2}$	Head lettuce, *or* to taste, shredded fine

Add an international flair to your menus with this traditional Middle Eastern dish.

❶ In large mixing bowl, add chopped onions and salt and mix well. Add juice of limes, olive oil, and mint.

❷ Soak bulgar wheat in hot water for 2 minutes. Drain well, squeeze out water. Add to the onion mixture and mix well. Add tomatoes, peppers, and cucumbers and toss well.

❸ Refrigerate to marinate for 2 hours. Toss the shredded lettuce into the salad just before serving.

MANGO AND GARBANZO TABOULI

Serves 4
Preparation time: 20 minutes
Soaking time: 30 minutes

R E C I P E   T I P S
Garbanzos—also called chickpeas—lend a hearty flavor to this unique version of fruit and curry tabouli. Vary the recipe by using $^{1}/_{2}$ cup orange juice in addition to the lime juice. Or add 1 small banana, sliced. Or toss in 3 tablespoons lightly toasted flaked coconut along with the raisins and nuts.

D O - A H E A D   T I P S
The bulgar wheat can be soaked up to a day ahead of time. Use canned garbanzos or prepare dried ones ahead of time. If you use Tofu Sour Cream, it can be made up to 3 days in advance and kept in the refrigerator.

◆

1	Cup coarse bulgar wheat
1	Cup boiling water
	Juice of $^{1}/_{2}$ lime
1	Ripe mango *or* 2 ripe peaches, peeled and chopped
1 - 2	Teaspoons curry powder, to taste
1	Cup precooked garbanzos
$^{1}/_{4}$	Cup raisins
$^{1}/_{4}$	Cup dry-roasted almonds *or* peanuts, chopped
$^{2}/_{3}$	Cup low-fat plain yogurt *or* Tofu Sour Cream (recipe in variation section)

❶ Pour the boiling water over the bulgar wheat. Cover and let stand until the water is absorbed, 20 to 30 minutes.

❷ Meanwhile, combine the lime juice, mango *or* peaches, and curry powder. Stir well to blend. Add the garbanzos, raisins, and almonds. Stir well.

❸ When the bulgar wheat has expanded and all the water is absorbed, add it to the other ingredients. Add the yogurt *or* Tofu Sour Cream and stir to coat evenly. Serve at room temperature or chilled.

Salad Dressings, Dips, and Flavored Oils

The following are some of my favorite salad dressing recipes. When the recipe calls for oil, add variety by choosing a flavored oil that will blend well with the other ingredients.

BELL PEPPER OIL

Makes $^1/_2$ cup
Preparation time: 20 minutes

R E C I P E   T I P S
This will make a thick, sweet, emulsified oil. Yellow peppers can also be used.

◆

4 - 5	Red *or* yellow bell peppers
$^1/_4$	Cup extra-virgin olive oil

❶ Put peppers through a juice extractor; they should yield about 1 cup of juice. In a small saucepan over low heat, steam until liquid is reduced by half; strain. Pour into a clean saucepan. Bring to a boil and simmer for 15-30 minutes, or until reduced to a syrup. There'll be about $^1/_4$ cup.

❷ Pour syrup into a small glass jar and add an equal amount (about $^1/_4$ cup) of olive oil. Cover and shake well; store in the refrigerator for up to 2 weeks. Shake before using.

BASIL-FLAVORED OIL

Preparation time: 10 minutes
Cooking time: 5 minutes

R E C I P E   T I P S
You can also use cilantro, oregano, dill, parsley, or mint to flavor the oil.

◆

$^1/_2$	Cup fresh basil leaves
	Olive oil

❶ Blanch basil leaves and some of the stems. Rinse under cold water; pat dry.

❷ Puree in a blender along with an equal amount of oil. Pour into a small glass jar and add twice as much oil as puree mixture. Cover and shake well.

❸ Refrigerate oil overnight. Bring back to room temperature and pour through a strainer lined with damp cheesecloth. Do not press on the solids. Refrigerate oil, covered, for up to 2 weeks.

GARLIC-FLAVORED OIL

Makes $^1/_2$ cup
Preparation time: 10 minutes

R E C I P E   T I P S
The garlic oil does not need to be strained for use in Italian sauces or recipes that have enough texture and are going to be cooked. For salad dressings, be sure to strain.

◆

3	Garlic cloves
$^1/_2$	Cup olive oil, canola oil, *or* basil oil (see recipe in flavored-oil section)

❶ Mince garlic or press through a garlic press with large holes so most of the garlic comes through. Place in $^1/_2$ cup oil. Let stand overnight. Strain out the minced garlic by pouring oil mixture through strainer lined with damp cheesecloth. Refrigerate oil, covered, for up to 4 weeks.

LEMON-GARLIC DRESSING

Serves 16   Makes 1 cup
Preparation time: 5 minutes

R E C I P E   T I P S
This light dressing adds a delicious flavor to salads and vegetables. Garlic-flavored oil can substitute for step 2. Try using other flavored oils as well. Make this recipe at least 1 hour before serving to allow flavors to blend at room temperature.

◆

$^1/_2$	Cup light olive oil, *or* flavored oil of your choice
$^1/_2$	Cup lemon juice
2 - 3	Garlic cloves, peeled, halved, and speared on a toothpick
	Salt to taste (optional)

❶ In small bowl, combine oil, lemon juice, and salt to taste.

❷ Drop in the toothpick-speared garlic and allow to stand at room temperature about 1 hour. Remove garlic just prior to serving.

GUACAMOLE

Serves 2
Preparation time: 5 minutes

R E C I P E   T I P S

Serve this recipe with tortilla chips, as a spread for a sandwich, or with your favorite Mexican meal.

———————— ◆ ————————

2	Avocados, peeled, pitted, and mashed
$^1/_2$	Small sweet onion, minced finely
$^1/_4$	Cup tomatoes, chopped fine (optional)
3	Tablespoons fresh squeezed lime juice with pulp
1	Teaspoon garlic salt

This is Wendy Bergman's guacamole recipe. The addition of fresh lime juice is her special touch.

❶ In small mixing bowl, combine avocado, onion, tomatoes, lime juice, and garlic salt. To prevent discoloring, cover top of dip with plastic wrap, taking care to remove all air. Chill and serve.

POPPY SEED DRESSING

Serves 16 Makes 1 cup
Preparation time: 10 minutes

R E C I P E   T I P S

This mouthwatering dressing will liven up the simplest tossed green salad. This dressing will last up to 10 days in the refrigerator.

———————— ◆ ————————

$^1/_4$	Cup small white onion, chopped
$^1/_4$	Cup honey
2 $^1/_2$	Tablespoons fresh lemon juice
$^1/_2$	Teaspoon dry mustard (optional)
$^1/_4$	Teaspoon salt (optional)
$^1/_2$	Cup light olive oil (*or* $^1/_4$ cup water *and* $^1/_4$ cup oil)
1	Tablespoon poppy seeds

❶ In blender or food processor, blend chopped onion on medium speed until slushy.

❷ Add honey and lemon juice to onion and blend. Add dry mustard and salt to taste if desired.

❸ With blender or food processor running on medium-high speed, slowly pour in oil or oil/water mixture. Mixture in blender will be thick and creamy. (If you use the oil/water mixture to lower the fat content, it will be slightly thinner, but still delicious.)

❹ Add poppy seeds and blend or process a few seconds longer, being careful that poppy seeds remain whole.

❺ Store in refrigerator until needed.

CREAMY CUCUMBER DRESSING

Makes 1 $^3/_4$ cups
Preparation time: 5 minutes

R E C I P E   T I P S

This recipe tastes delicious over your favorite tossed green salad or as a vegetable dip. After refrigerating, the mixture thickens and is the perfect consistency for a vegetable dip. Thin if desired by mixing in a small amount of water.

D O - A H E A D   T I P S

This dressing keeps up to 5 days in the refrigerator.

———————— ◆ ————————

1	Cup tofu, mashed
1	Medium cucumber, peeled and chopped
2	Tablespoons olive oil
2	Tablespoons lemon juice
$^1/_2$	Teaspoon salt
1	Teaspoon fresh dill, chopped, *or* $^1/_2$ teaspoon dried dill

❶ In blender container, blend all above ingredients until smooth and creamy. Serve chilled over salad.

Dressings

HUMMUS DIP

Serves 6-8
Preparation time: 5 minutes

R E C I P E   T I P S
Serve with toasted pita bread wedges as an appetizer or with a tabouli salad as a light lunch.

◆

1	15-ounce can garbanzos
$^1/_4$	Cup tahini (sesame paste)
4	Tablespoons lemon juice
2	Large garlic cloves, peeled and cut in thirds
$^1/_4$	Teaspoon ground cumin
	Salt to taste
	Olive oil to drizzle
	Parsley for garnish

❶ Drain garbanzos, reserving liquid. In blender or food processor container, combine garbanzos, tahini, lemon juice, garlic, cumin, and $^1/_4$ cup reserved garbanzo liquid. Blend, adding more garbanzo liquid if needed, until mixture is smooth and the consistency of heavy batter. Season to taste with salt if desired.

❷ Serve chilled, drizzled with olive oil and sprinkled with parsley.

TAHINI DRESSING

Makes 1 $^1/_2$ cups (24 1-tablespoon servings)
Preparation time: 5 minutes

R E C I P E   T I P S
Try this recipe served over a pita bread sandwich filled with salad greens or drizzled on top of your favorite vegetables or salad. This recipe can be kept in the refrigerator for one week. The flavor improves after the second day.

◆

$^1/_2$	Cup purchased tahini (sesame seed paste)
or $^1/_2$	Cup **Homemade Tahini** (recipe following)
$^1/_4$	Cup water

$^1/_2$	Cup plain low-fat yogurt
or $^1/_2$	Cup **Tofu Sour Cream** (recipe in variation section)
2	Tablespoons fresh lemon juice
2	Small cloves fresh garlic, crushed

❶ In blender, combine all ingredients and blend until smooth.

Homemade Tahini:

2	Cups sesame seeds
$^1/_4$	Cup olive oil *or* other vegetable oil

❶ Place seeds in blender or nut grinder and grind to a fine powder. Add oil slowly, blending constantly, until mixture reaches the consistency of peanut butter. Use in tahini dressing recipe or as a butter or dip.

LIGHT VINAIGRETTE

Serves 7 - Makes $^1/_2$ cup
Preparation time: 8 minutes

R E C I P E   T I P S
Spoon this fat-free dressing over sliced or cut-up vegetables or salad greens. Vary by adding any of the following: 2 cloves garlic, minced; $^1/_4$ teaspoon dried tarragon, basil, oregano, or thyme, crushed; $^1/_4$ teaspoon dried dill weed.

D O - A H E A D   T I P S
This dressing will last up to 2 weeks in the refrigerator.

◆

1	Tablespoon powdered pectin
2	Teaspoons sugar *or* honey
$^1/_4$	Teaspoon salt *or* garlic powder
$^1/_8$	Teaspoon dry mustard
$^1/_4$	Cup water
2	Tablespoons lemon juice

❶ In screw-top jar, combine pectin, sugar, salt, and dry mustard. Add water and lemon juice. Cover and shake till blended. Let stand 3 to 4 minutes to dissolve pectin. Shake again. Store in refrigerator for up to 2 weeks.

Dressings

SPICY CITRUS DRESSING

Serves 7   Makes $1/2$ cup
Preparation time: 5 minutes

R E C I P E   T I P S

Drizzle over mixed fruit, with or without salad greens. Vary with any of the following: $1/2$ teaspoon poppy seeds or sesame seeds, dash of hot pepper sauce, or $1/2$ teaspoon ground ginger.

D O - A H E A D   T I P S

Dressing will last up to 2 weeks in the refrigerator.

◆

$1/4$	Cup lemon *or* lime juice
1	Tablespoon canola vegetable oil
2	Tablespoons honey
$1/4$	Teaspoon ground cinnamon, allspice, *or* cardamom
$1/8$	Teaspoon paprika

❶ In a screw-top jar, combine all dressing ingredients and shake well. Chill. Shake before serving.

ITALIAN HERB DRESSING

Serves 16   Makes 1 cup (1 tablespoon per serving)
Preparation time: 5 minutes

R E C I P E   T I P S

Any combination of herbs will be great in this salad dressing. Also, try some of the flavored oils to add variety. Make this dressing up to 2 weeks ahead and store in refrigerator.

◆

$1/3$	Cup water
$1/3$	Cup light olive oil *or* canola oil
$1/8$	Cup fresh lemon juice
1	Small garlic clove, crushed, *or* $1/4$ teaspoon garlic powder
$1/8$	Teaspoon dried *or* 1 teaspoon fresh basil

$1/8$	Teaspoon dried *or* 1 teaspoon fresh oregano
$1/8$	Teaspoon dried *or* 1 teaspoon fresh parsley
$1/4$	Teaspoon sugar *or* honey

Salt to taste (optional)

❶ In screw-top jar, combine all dressing ingredients. Chill until ready to serve. Shake before each use.

APRICOT YOGURT DRESSING

Serves 20   Makes 1-$1/4$ cups
Preparation time: 5-10 minutes

R E C I P E   T I P S

This dressing tastes great with the Waldorf "Chicken" Salad Pitas in place of the yogurt dressing in the recipe.

D O - A H E A D   T I P S

This dressing can be made up to one week ahead and refrigerated.

◆

1	Cup plain low-fat yogurt *or* Tofu Sour Cream (recipe in variation section)
$1/4$	Cup dried apricots, coarsely chopped
3	Tablespoons safflower oil
2	Tablespoons lemon juice
1	Teaspoon honey
1	Teaspoon onion, minced
1	Teaspoon celery seed (optional)

Salt to taste (optional)

❶ In food processor or blender, blend yogurt or Tofu Sour Cream and apricots until smooth. Stir in oil, lemon juice, honey, and onion. Add celery seed and salt if desired. Chill briefly before serving.

Dressings

CREAMY BASIL DRESSING

Serves 16   Makes 1 cup
Preparation time: 5 minutes

R E C I P E   T I P S

The thin version of this recipe makes a great salad dressing. When thickened after refrigeration it makes a good vegetable dip, topping for a baked potato, or mayonnaise replacement for sandwiches.

D O - A H E A D   T I P S

This recipe tastes best after marinating in the refrigerator for 24 hours. It will last 7 to 10 days in the refrigerator. You may need to thin this dressing just before serving if it is too thick.

◆

3	Tablespoons lemon juice
1 $^1/_2$	Tablespoons fresh basil, chopped,
or $^1/_2$	Tablespoon dried basil
$^1/_2$	Teaspoon dry mustard (optional)
1	Medium garlic clove, minced
3	Tablespoons olive *or* safflower oil
$^3/_4$	Cup plain low-fat yogurt
or $^3/_4$	Cup soft tofu, broken into pieces

❶ In food processor or blender, combine the lemon juice, basil, mustard, and garlic. Process until smooth. Then, with machine running, gradually add oil. When oil has been completely blended in, add tofu (if making nondairy option) and blend until smooth. If using yogurt, remove the dressing from the food processor and place in small bowl and gently stir in yogurt.

❷ Season to taste with salt. Cover and refrigerate. Stir well before each serving. The tofu version will thicken when chilled. Thin with a teaspoon or so of water if needed.

RANCH DRESSING (NONDAIRY)

Serves 20   Makes 1$^1/_4$ cups (1 tablespoon per serving)
Preparation time: 10 minutes

R E C I P E   T I P S

This recipe is a great replacement for ranch dressing or as a spread on bread to replace mayonnaise. For a vegetable dip, just leave the dressing thick after it has set up from being chilled. Serve as a sour cream replacement for baked potatoes.

D O - A H E A D   T I P S

This dressing can be stored for 7-10 days in the refrigerator.

◆

1	Cup soft tofu, broken into small pieces
2	Tablespoons light olive, canola, *or* a flavored oil
4	Teaspoons fresh lemon juice
$^1/_4$ - $^1/_2$	Teaspoon dried *or* 1 - 2 teaspoons fresh dill weed
$^1/_4$	Teaspoon salt
1	Small garlic clove, pressed *or* minced

❶ In blender, combine all ingredients and blend until smooth and creamy. Chill before serving. Add more water to thin dressing down if it is too thick after chilling.

A zesty, creamy dressing that tastes great served as a salad dressing, sandwich spread, or topping for a baked potato.

Dressings

D I N N E R

VEGETARIAN FAJITAS
This Mexican speciality has siz-
zling good taste–and is low in fat
and cholesterol.

Recipe on page 69

Main Meals in Minutes

The easiest option at the end of a hectic day is often the nearest fast-food restaurant. But we're changing the way we think about food, and many of us are deciding that serving healthful, home-cooked meals is more important than fast-food convenience. Now that we've changed our thinking, we need quick and easy recipes that will keep us healthy while fitting into our busy lifestyles.

Help! I'm too busy to cook healthy!

A common complaint I often hear at cooking seminars is, "We understand the importance of cutting the fat, cholesterol, and sodium in our diets, but only those who don't work have the time to make all these healthful meals from scratch!"

These dinner recipes take on this challenge. They assume that you don't plan to spend your days in the kitchen—that you often get home from work with nothing planned for dinner—and no time to prepare elaborate meals. Now you can have healthful dinners that are deliciously low in fat and a breeze to fix.

Relax and enjoy the extra time saved in meal preparation.

CHINESE CASHEW CASSEROLE

Serves 6
Preparation time: 10 minutes
Cooking time: 30 minutes

M E N U   T I P S

The approval of your taste buds will put this Chinese dish on your list of favorites. The ease of preparation will put it at the top of the list. This recipe is great for potluck dinners or other occasions. Serve it with whole grain rice and your choice of cooked vegetables for a complete healthful meal. For a really special occasion, add Worthington FriChik® Wontons (recipe following).

D O - A H E A D   T I P S

This dish can be made ahead and refrigerated either before or after baking. Just reheat in oven until it is warmed throughout and the top is lightly browned.

◆

1   Cup celery, chopped, *or* 1 cup water chestnuts, chopped

1   Large onion, chopped

1   Cup cashew nuts, halved *or* whole

1   Cup dried Chinese noodles

1   Cup fine egg noodles, uncooked

1   Can mushroom soup, undiluted

❶ In large mixing bowl, first mix together all ingredients except mushroom soup. Then add mushroom soup and mix gently to evenly coat dry mixture.

❷ Spray oven-proof casserole dish with nonstick vegetable spray. Add cashew mixture. Bake at 350° F for 30 minutes or until lightly browned on top. Serve.

This recipe comes from my good friend Chai Mau, who also taught me the Oriental secrets of making great tofu and rice dishes.

FRICHIK WONTONS

Serves 16   Makes 32 wontons
Preparation time: 20 minutes
Cooking time: 20 minutes

R E C I P E   T I P S

These wontons take a little extra time. You may want to save them for special-occasion meals. Look for Worthington FriChik in health food stores or some supermarkets. It comes in a can, and is a tender, juicy, healthful alternative to chicken, made from textured wheat gluten. Buy wonton skins at an Oriental market or your local supermarket.

D O - A H E A D   T I P S

These wontons can be made ahead, then baked and frozen for later use. Just recrisp or reheat in oven.

◆

1   12.5-ounce can Worthington FriChik®, drained

1   Small onion, finely chopped

1   Carrot, peeled and grated fine

$1/2$ Cup water chestnuts, chopped fine

1   Teaspoon McKay's Chicken-Style Seasoning

32   Wonton skins

❶ In food processor, chop well-drained FriChik until very fine. Place in a small mixing bowl.

❷ In food processor or by hand: finely chop the onion and add to FriChik. Add the grated carrot, chopped water chestnuts, and McCay's Chicken-Style Seasoning. Mix well.

❸ To assemble: Place wonton square on flat surface and put 1 teaspoon of filling in the center. Brush the edges of the wonton lightly with water. Fold the bottom corner up to meet the top corner, making a triangle, and seal edges. This shape is best for browning the wontons evenly if you are sautéing or baking them. For a fancier design, pull the outside corners together and twist slightly.

❹ To cook: Spray wontons and nonstick skillet with nonstick vegetable spray. Add wontons to skillet and cook on medium-high temperature, turning after 2-3 minutes when wontons are lightly browned and crunchy. Or put wontons sprayed with nonstick spray on cookie sheet also sprayed with nonstick vegetable spray and bake in 450° F oven until lightly browned, approximately 10 minutes per side. Another option is to drop folded wontons in boiling water for approximately 10 minutes and serve in a soft form like a stuffed pasta shell. Serve both the crisp or soft wontons immediately after cooking.

Make plenty of these crunchy and healthy treats; you and your guests may have a hard time resisting seconds.

ORIENTAL PEPPER STEAK OVER RICE

Serves 8
Preparation time: 20 minutes
Sauce cooking time: 15 minutes
Rice cooking time: 35 minutes

R E C I P E   T I P S

This recipe tastes great served over rice, but it is equally good over oven-toasted Italian bread or thin egg noodles. Add a fresh-cooked vegetable for a nutritionally balanced meal.

D O - A H E A D   T I P S

The rice can be prepared in the morning and kept warm if you are using a rice cooker. You also can let the tofu drain in the refrigerator all day to extract as much liquid as possible. When you get home in the evening, all you need to do is make the sauce.

◆

4	Cups whole-grain rice, uncooked
or 8	Cups cooked rice
1	1-pound block firm tofu
1	Large onion, chopped
1	Green pepper, sliced thin
2	Cloves garlic, minced fine *or* pressed in a garlic press
6	Mushrooms, sliced
1	Quart canned whole tomatoes, crushed
2	Tablespoons light soy sauce
or 1	Heaping tablespoon miso (soybean paste)

❶ Prepare rice according to the directions on page 10.

❷ Drain tofu. (Place tofu on something absorbent, such as folded paper towels. Weight down with something heavy, such as a plastic container filled with water, to extract as much water as possible. Leave it like this overnight or all day in the refrigerator or for as long as possible before cooking. The more liquid you extract, the better the tofu's texture in this recipe.)

❸ Cut the drained tofu block in strips parallel to the short side of the block. Make approximately 5 or 6 thick slices. Sauté tofu strips in nonstick skillet, sprayed with nonstick vegetable spray until both sides are lightly browned. Set aside.

❹ In skillet, sauté onion, green pepper, garlic, and mushrooms in a little oil until softened. Add crushed tomatoes and soy sauce or miso and bring to a boil. Then add browned tofu strips and let simmer gently for 5 minutes. Serve over rice.

ORIENTAL TOFU-PEANUT SAUCE OVER RICE

Serves 4
Preparation time: 10 minutes
Sauce cooking time: 10 minutes
Rice cooking time: 35 minutes

R E C I P E   T I P S

Give this recipe a try—it has a wonderful flavor. You can also serve this sauce over cooked thin egg noodles or oven-toasted bread.

D O - A H E A D   T I P S

If you are using a heavy pot, the rice can be cooked in the morning and left covered on the stove until serving time.

◆

2	Cups whole-grain rice, uncooked, *or* 4 cups cooked rice *or* one package thin egg noodles
1	Small onion, chopped
1	Clove garlic, minced
1	Pound soft tofu, drained
2	Tablespoons crunchy peanut butter
2	Tablespoons light soy sauce
1 - 2	Scallions, chopped fine

❶ Make rice according to directions on page 10, *or* prepare noodles according to package directions.

❷ In skillet, sauté onion and garlic in a little oil until softened.

❸ Drain tofu and crumble into sautéed mixture.

❹ Stir in peanut butter and soy sauce. Bring to a gentle simmer.

❺ Add chopped scallions and simmer 1 to 2 minutes more.

❻ Serve immediately over rice *or* noodles.

Another famous fix-it-fast Oriental recipe from Chai Mau

You won't believe this rich, creamy à la King sauce contains no oil! Ladle it generously over noodles or rice.

"CHICKEN" à la KING

Serves 6
Preparation time: 20 minutes
Cooking time: 30-35 minutes

M E N U   T I P S
Serve this "Chicken" à la King with a simple tossed green salad and whole-grain bread. Loma Linda Tender Bits are a canned vegetable protein, made from wheat gluten, available in most natural food stores and some supermarkets. They are a good choice in dishes that call for chicken. If you prefer, you may substitute garbanzos for the Tender Bits. This one-dish meal is also delicious when served over egg noodles or toast.

D O - A H E A D   T I P S
The sauce can be made the day before and refrigerated in an airtight container. If you have a rice cooker, you can prepare the rice in the morning before leaving home and it will stay warm until dinner. Then when you come home all you need to do is heat up the sauce and pour it over the rice.

◆

Rice:
4	Cups long-grain brown rice
$^1/_4$ - $^1/_2$	Cup wild rice (optional)
6	Cups water
2	Packages G. Washington Broth mix, Golden
or 2	Tablespoons McKay's Chicken-Style Seasoning

Sautéed Vegetable Mixture:
1	Cup onions, chopped
1	Red or green pepper, chopped
2	Cups Loma Linda® Tender Bits, sliced
$^1/_2$	Cup mushrooms, sliced
2	Tablespoons canola oil

Sauce:
3	Cups of water or garbanzo liquid (if using garbanzos)
$^1/_2$	Cup cashew pieces
4	Tablespoons sesame seeds
2 - 3	Tablespoons McKay's Chicken-Style Seasoning
$^1/_4$	Teaspoon salt (optional)
$^3/_4$	Teaspoon garlic powder
1	Tablespoon onion powder
1	Tablespoon cornstarch
1	Cup carrots, sliced and blanched
3	Cups frozen peas
2	Cups cooked garbanzos (eliminate these if using Tender Bits)
$^1/_2$	Cup blanched slivered almonds (optional)

❶ As an option, the rice can be toasted before cooking for an added distinct, nutty flavor. See directions on page 10.

❷ If using a rice cooker, place water, George Washington Broth mix, rice and wild rice, if desired, in cooker. Turn it on and it will automatically cook the rice to perfection in 30 to 35 minutes. If using a heavy saucepan, bring the 6 cups of water to a boil and then add the rice, wild rice if desired, and seasoning. Return to a boil, then lower temperature to the lowest setting and simmer covered for 35 to 40 minutes or until rice is thoroughly cooked.

❸ While rice is cooking, start the sauce. In a skillet, sauté in the oil the chopped onion, red pepper, mushrooms, and Tender Bits until vegetables are softened and Tender Bits are lightly browned. Set aside.

❹ In blender, combine 3 cups of water or garbanzo liquid, cashews, sesame seeds, McKay's seasoning, salt, garlic powder, onion powder, and cornstarch. Blend several minutes until mixture is smooth.

❺ Pour the blender mixture into the sautéed vegetable-and-Tender Bit mixture and bring to a boil over medium heat. Let simmer approximately 5 minutes or until sauce thickens. Add blanched carrots, frozen peas, and almonds if desired. Add garbanzos if not using Tender Bits.
Note: You may want to add some chopped canned pimentos for color, if you used green pepper in the sautéed mixture.) Heat sauce thoroughly.

My friend Sue invited me over for dinner and served Chickpea à la King. It was so delicious that I adapted it into this "Chicken" à la King recipe.

❻ **To assemble:**
On large platter spread rice about 2 inches thick and pour all the sauce over the rice. Garnish with red and green peppers and serve immediately. Make sure there is plenty of sauce to flavor all the rice.

TOSTADA CLUB

Serves 1
Preparation time: 15 minutes
Cooking time: 15 minutes

R E C I P E   T I P S

This recipe uses carrots—in place of cheddar cheese—vegetarian beans, and Tofu Sour Cream for a wonderful Mexican dinner with zero cholesterol and very little fat. Use precooked canned beans to save time.

D O - A H E A D   T I P S

If you are cooking the beans from scratch, they can be done several days ahead of time. The lettuce, tomatoes, carrots, and onion can be chopped ahead and refrigerated for 1 to 2 days.

◆

2	Flour tortillas
$^1/_2$	Cup black beans, cooked
3	Tablespoons green chilies
$^1/_4$	Teaspoon cumin
	Garlic powder to taste
$^1/_2$	Cup vegetarian chili beans *or* refried beans
1	Cup iceberg lettuce, shredded
$^1/_2$	Cup tomatoes, chopped
$^1/_2$	Cup carrots, grated
1	Tablespoon scallions, chopped
2	Tablespoons **Tofu Sour Cream** (recipe in variation section) *or* low-fat sour cream
$^1/_4$	Cup Guacamole (recipe in salad dressing section)
	Mild *or* hot picante sauce to taste

❶ In nonstick skillet over high heat, place flour tortilla and toast until just crispy on each side. Repeat with remaining tortilla.

❷ On large oven-proof plate, place one tortilla. Spread black beans thinly over entire tortilla. Sprinkle with green chilies, cumin, and garlic powder. Top this with remaining tortilla. Spread with thin layer of chili beans or refried beans. Place the plate in 450° F oven for approximately 10 minutes or until bean mixture begins to bubble. Remove from oven.

❸ Add a layer of shredded lettuce, tomatoes, carrots, and scallions. In the center place a scoop of Tofu Sour Cream or low-fat sour cream and a scoop of guacamole. Garnish with picante sauce to taste. Serve.

ZUCCHINI "CRAB" CAKES

Serves 6   Makes 12 to 14 "crab" cakes
Preparation time: 15 minutes
Cooking time: 15 minutes

M E N U   T I P S

Old Bay Seasoning is a blend of herbs and spices for seafood, which originated in the Chesapeake Bay area, where I live. Serve this recipe with Sweet and Sour Sauce or Low-Fat Tartar Sauce from the variation section. Serve as an appetizer or on a kaiser roll with tartar sauce for lunch or as a light supper.

D O - A H E A D   T I P S

Make these cakes ahead of time and refrigerate or freeze them. When you arrive home in the evening, just reheat them in the microwave or oven and serve with a steamed vegetable or tossed green salad.

◆

	2	Cups zucchini, coarsely grated
	4	Egg whites, beaten
or	$^1/_2$	Cup soft tofu, blended
or	$^1/_2$	Cup egg substitute, such as Morningstar Farms® Scramblers
	1	Cup seasoned bread crumbs
	2	Tablespoons low-fat mayonnaise *or* **Soy Mayonnaise** (recipe in variation section)
	1 $^1/_2$	Teaspoons Old Bay Seasoning

❶ In medium-sized mixing bowl, combine zucchini, egg whites, tofu, *or* egg substitute, bread crumbs, mayonnaise or soy mayonnaise, and Old Bay Seasoning. Mix thoroughly.

Jane Lanning developed this recipe–a great vegetarian version of traditional crab cakes.

❷ Form into golf-ball sized balls and roll lightly in additional bread crumbs.

❸ In nonstick skillet over medium-high temperature, place a small amount of oil. Place "crab" cake balls in skillet and pat the balls lightly with a spoon to form a thick patty. Lightly brown both sides. Serve with tartar sauce *or* sweet and sour sauce. See recipes for sauces in variation section.

VEGETARIAN FAJITAS

Serves 8
Preparation time: 15 minutes
Cooking time: 10 minutes

M E N U   T I P S

If you love Mexican food but need to cut the cholesterol and fat in your diet, this recipe is just for you. Worthington Stakelets® are a tasty addition to this recipe. Look for them in the freezer section of your natural food store or supermarket. For a complete meal, add rice to the tortilla, or serve fajitas with a side dish of rice.

D O - A H E A D   T I P S

Fajitas always taste best when served immediately.

◆

Sautéed Stakelets and Vegetables:

1	10-ounce package Worthington Stakelets, thawed
2	Tablespoons vegetable oil
1	Cup onion, sliced
$^1/_2$	Cup green pepper, sliced
$^1/_2$	Cup red pepper, sliced

Seasoning Mix:

1	Tablespoon garlic powder
1	Tablespoon chili powder
1	Teaspoon paprika
1	Teaspoon dried basil

Toppings for Fajitas:

$^1/_2$	Cup tomatoes, chopped
2	Cups lettuce, shredded
$^1/_4$	Cup avocado, peeled and chopped
$^1/_4$	Cup low-fat sour cream *or* **Tofu Sour Cream** (recipe in variation section)
8	Flour tortillas
	Hot *or* mild salsa, to taste

❶ In small bowl, mix together ingredients to make seasoning mix. Cut Stakelets into strips. Sprinkle the Stakelets strips with the seasoning mix.

❷ Heat large skillet until very hot. Add oil and sauté onion and pepper until tender. Add Stakelets and cook until Stakelets are heated and slightly crisp.

❸ Place about 2 ounces of sautéed Stakelets mixture on each flour tortilla and top with the chopped tomato, lettuce, avocado, and sour cream. Roll up tortilla and serve immediately with hot *or* mild salsa.   *Pictured on page 62*

VEGETARIAN "FILLET OF FISH" OVER RICE

Serves 6
Total preparation: 10 minutes
Cooking time: 10 minutes
Rice cooking time: 35 minutes

R E C I P E   T I P S

This vegetarian version of "fish" uses Worthington "fish" Fillets. This non-meat product comes frozen and can be found at most natural food stores.

D O - A H E A D   T I P S

To get this meal on the table fast, make the rice ahead of time, or serve over something quicker to prepare, such as toast or noodles.

◆

3	Cups whole-grain rice, uncooked, *or* 6 cups cooked rice
1	Onion, chopped
1	Pound firm tofu, drained
2	Worthington "fish" Fillets
1	Can mushroom soup, undiluted

❶ In skillet, sauté the onion in a little oil until soft. Crumble the drained tofu and the two "fish" fillets into the skillet and brown lightly.

❷ Add mushroom soup and simmer until moisture is somewhat absorbed by the tofu and fillets. Serve warm over a 1 cup serving of rice.

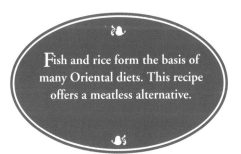

Fish and rice form the basis of many Oriental diets. This recipe offers a meatless alternative.

Baked garlic is the succulent center of attraction in this deep-dish vegetable pinwheel.

GARLIC-HERB VEGETABLE BAKE

Serves 4
Preparation time: 10 minutes
Baking time: 30-40 minutes

R E C I P E   T I P S

This recipe can be made with a variety of vegetables. The vegetables in this recipe cook quicker than other vegetable combinations and the thin vegetable slices are overlapped and laid in strips for quicker cooking. Make a deep-dish version by layering longer-cooking vegetables on the bottom of a deep casserole dish and the quickest cooking vegetables closer to the top. Plan on extra baking time if you use this method, especially if you use vegetables that have less moisture, like carrots, broccoli, and cauliflower. Add fresh herbs and garlic slices to the deep dish version; cover and bake approximately 1 hour.

D O - A H E A D   T I P S

This recipe tastes best straight out of the oven. You can prepare and cut the vegetables ahead for last-minute assembly.

◆

2	Zucchini, thinly sliced
2	Large tomatoes, thinly sliced
2	Baking potatoes, thinly sliced
10	Garlic cloves, thinly sliced
1	Whole garlic bulb, with outside skins removed and tops to each clove cut off
2	Tablespoons olive oil
10	Fresh basil leaves, chopped

❶ Preheat oven to 400° F. Arrange vegetables in a lightly oiled shallow 12-inch circular casserole dish. Place the whole garlic bulb in the center of the casserole dish and alternate the slices of vegetables around it in overlapping circles. Sprinkle with thin garlic slices and chopped basil leaves.

❷. Lightly brush the vegetables with olive oil and bake for 30 to 40 minutes, or until potatoes are tender.

❸ Garnish with fresh whole basil leaves if desired. Sprinkle with salt or garlic powder to taste. If you baked the whole garlic bulb, then spread the garlic paste from each clove on the vegetables or on toasted bread slices.

This recipe was adapted from a dish my husband's sister, Beth Schock, made for a family dinner—an unforgettable, mouthwatering creation.

HERBED VEGETABLE ENCHILADAS

Serves 6-8   Makes 12 enchiladas
Preparation time: 20 minutes
Cooking time: 15 minutes

R E C I P E   T I P S
This saucy cheese-free enchilada is stuffed with sautéed vegetables. The spinach is optional, but adds great flavor.

D O - A H E A D   T I P S
To make ahead, cover and refrigerate prepared dish of enchiladas for up to 24 hours. This dish also freezes well.

◆

12	6- or 8-inch corn tortillas
2	Cups tomato juice
1	Teaspoon cumin
1	Teaspoon garlic powder

Filling:

1	Tablespoon olive oil *or* 1 tablespoon water
1	Large onion, chopped
2	Garlic cloves, minced
1	Can green chilies, chopped
$^1/_2$	Cup carrots, grated fine
$^1/_2$	Cup zucchini, grated fine
1	Cup fresh spinach, torn in bite-sized pieces
or 1	Cup frozen spinach, chopped and thawed
2	Tablespoons fresh cilantro *or* parsley (*or* 2 teaspoons dried)
2	Cups **Tofu Sour Cream** (recipe in variation section)
or 2	Cups low-fat sour cream
1	Cup tomatoes, chopped fine
$^1/_2$	Teaspoon salt (optional)
4	Cups **Spanish Sauce** (recipe following)

❶ Spray a 3-quart rectangular baking dish with nonstick vegetable spray and set aside.

❷ In large skillet sauté onions, garlic, green chilies, carrots, and zucchini in oil or cover and steam in water. Cook until vegetables are just tender. Add cilantro *or* parsley and spinach leaves and heat just until spinach leaves are wilted.

❸ Add to sautéed vegetable mixture: Tofu Sour Cream *or* low-fat sour cream, tomatoes, and salt. Set filling aside.

❹ In large skillet, warm tomato juice, add cumin and garlic powder, mix thoroughly. Dip tortillas in seasoned tomato juice to soften and stack them on top of each other on a plate.

❺ Spoon $^1/_2$ cup filling down the center of each tortilla; roll up. Arrange tortillas, seam side down, in the prepared baking dish.

❻ Prepare the Spanish Sauce and pour over enchiladas.

❼ Cover and bake in a 350° F oven for 15 minutes or till heated through.

SPANISH SAUCE

Makes 4 cups
Preparation time: 10 minutes
Cooking time: 8 minutes

R E C I P E   T I P S
Serve this sauce over enchiladas or burritos for a wonderful spicy flavor.

D O - A H E A D   T I P S
This sauce can be made several days in advance and warmed just before serving.

◆

$^1/_4$	Cup onion, chopped
$^1/_4$	Cup green pepper, chopped
$^1/_2$	Cup celery, sliced thin
1	Teaspoon canola *or* olive oil
or 2	Tablespoons water
$^1/_2$	Teaspoon chili powder
1	Teaspoon garlic powder
1	Cup canned tomatoes
2	Cups water
$2^1/_2$	Teaspoons sugar *or* honey
1	Tablespoon cold water
1	Teaspoon cornstarch

❶ In large skillet, sauté onion, green pepper, and celery in oil *or* cover and steam in water until just tender.

❷ Add chili powder and garlic powder to the sautéed vegetables. Add tomatoes, water, and sweetener to vegetable mixture and bring to a boil.

❸ In a cup mix 1 tablespoon water with cornstarch until cornstarch is dissolved completely. Pour this dissolved cornstarch mixture into the vegetable mixture and bring to a boil for 2 to 3 minutes. Mixture will thicken. Serve hot over enchiladas.

This recipe was adapted from one of my husband's sister, Cindy Mulflur's gourmet specialties. Her meals are always memorable.

TUSCANY-STYLE PASTA

Serves 6-8
Preparation time: 20 minutes
Cooking time: 10 minutes

M E N U   T I P S

This is a good dish to prepare for unexpected company. Just add a tossed green salad and toasted Italian bread and you have a complete meal in no more than 30 minutes.

D O - A H E A D   T I P S

You can roast several peppers at once and store them in the refrigerator for use in sauces, salads, sandwiches, and garnishes. Or you can purchase roasted whole red peppers in the jar in the specialty foods department of your supermarket. Look for capers in the same section. This dish can be made ahead of time and rewarmed, covered, in the oven or microwave.

1	Pound angel hair pasta
1	Tablespoon light olive oil *or* water
10 - 12	Garlic cloves, sliced very thin
1	Cup mushrooms, sliced thin
1	Cup fresh basil leaves, chopped, or 1 4.5-ounce jar of water-packed fresh basil *or* 2 tablespoon dried basil leaves
3	Tablespoons capers
1	Red pepper, roasted, peeled, and chopped
1	Cup unsalted sundried tomatoes, rehydrated and chopped
1	Cup fresh tomatoes, chopped
2	Cups carrots, thinly sliced diagonally (optional)

❶ **To roast pepper:** Using tongs, hold the pepper over a gas flame or broil it until the skin is black and loose. Place it in a sealed plastic bag for 20 minutes to steam. Remove skin and chop pepper.

❷ In large saucepan, start the water for the pasta. While this water is coming to a boil begin making the sautéed vegetable mixture.

❸ In large skillet over medium-high temperature sauté garlic cloves until tender. Turn temperature down a little and add mushrooms. Cook until they are tender. Toss in the basil, capers, chopped roasted peppers, rehydrated dried tomatoes, and fresh tomatoes and heat thoroughly. Set aside.

❹ Add pasta and carrots to boiling water and cook for 3 to 5 minutes or until the pasta is just tender. (Make sure the carrots are sliced on the diagonal and very thinly. If not, they won't cook to the perfect al dente stage in this short amount of time.) Drain pasta and carrots in colander.

❺ Pour half of the drained pasta and carrots back into the pan they were cooked in and add part of the garlic-vegetable sauce. Toss well to coat pasta evenly. Then add the remaining pasta and carrots and garlic-vegetable sauce and toss well again to coat all pasta. Serve immediately in large pasta bowl or on individual plates.

This deceptively simple main-
dish Italian creation will have your
friends and family coming back
for more.

PASTA G VIOLA

Serves 4-5
Preparation time: 10 minutes
Cooking time: 10 minutes

M E N U   T I P S
Serve this dish with fresh steamed broccoli and Italian bread and you have an authentic Italian meal. Or for a colorful variation, add small broccoli pieces or carrots to the sauce when you add the beans. Simmer until the vegetables are just tender. The secret to good Pasta g Viola is to be sure that the bean sauce is nice and juicy (thin it with water if necessary), and that you use a fine pasta such as angel hair, placed in a thin layer on the plate, with a generous portion of bean sauce.

D O - A H E A D   T I P S
This bean sauce can be made up to 2 days in advance and refrigerated until serving time. Just reheat in the microwave or in a skillet and serve over the hot pasta of your choice.

◆

1	Pound vermicelli *or* angel hair pasta
2	Tablespoons light olive oil
1	Large onion, chopped
10	Garlic cloves, minced
4	Cups precooked cannolini beans *or* white kidney beans, undrained
	Salt to taste if desired
	Parmesan cheese, for garnish if desired

❶ In a large saucepan, start water for pasta.

❷ In large skillet, combine olive oil and onion and cook over high heat until the onion is lightly browned. Add garlic and cook gently for an additional 3 minutes, but do not brown onion or garlic any further. Add precooked beans with liquid and return to a boil. Lower temperature and simmer for 5 minutes. (Additional water can be added to this sauce at this time if necessary). Add salt to taste, if desired.

❸ Put pasta in boiling water during the 5 minutes that the bean sauce is simmering. Cook pasta to the al dente stage and drain. On individual plates put a thin layer of pasta and top with a generous portion of bean sauce. Be sure to drizzle the bean liquid over the pasta to add flavor. Sprinkle lightly with Parmesan cheese, if desired, and serve immediately. This dish tastes wonderful without any cheese.

An Italian friend, Gail Depuy, first served me this traditional Italian dish. I was skeptical, but took a bite to be polite. To my surprise, it was wonderful. This low-fat adaptation is now on our family-favorite list.

ZUCCHINI ZITI

Serves 6-8
Preparation time: 15 minutes
Cooking time: 15 minutes

M E N U   T I P S

This ziti dish does not require baking like the traditional baked ziti, so it saves time. It also contains no cheese, so it is low in cholesterol and fat. Serve with a tossed salad or steamed vegetable and crusty hard bread. To vary the recipe, try adding 2 cups of canned Italian cannolini beans in place of the Loma Linda Tender Bits.

D O - A H E A D   T I P S

This sauce can be made ahead and warmed up. Pour on top the freshly prepared pasta before serving. For a potluck or party, you can toss the sauce with the pasta, put in a nonstick covered baking dish and refrigerate for several days. Before serving, reheat the pasta in a 350° F oven for about 30 minutes or till heated thoroughly.

◆

1	Pound ziti pasta
1	Tablespoon light olive oil, *or* water
1	Large onion, chopped
4	Garlic cloves, minced
1	19-ounce can Loma Linda® Tender Bits, sliced
2	Zucchini squash, halved lengthwise and sliced
3	14.5-ounce cans (6 cups) chopped tomatoes
or 6	Cups fresh tomatoes, chopped
	Pinch of sugar, to taste
1	Teaspoon lemon juice
2	Teaspoons dried basil
1	Teaspoon dried oregano
	Salt to taste (optional)

❶ In large saucepan, start enough water for pasta.

❷ In large skillet, sauté in olive oil *or* steam in water the chopped onion until just tender. Add garlic cloves and Tender Bits and continue cooking until Tender Bits are lightly browned. Add zucchini and cook until just tender. Mix in tomatoes, sugar, lemon juice, basil, oregano, and optional salt and simmer for an additional 5 minutes. Set aside.

❸ Add ziti to boiling water when you add the tomatoes to the sautéed mixture. Cook pasta for approximately 8 minutes or until just tender. Drain and put back in saucepan.

❹ On individual plates place a layer of pasta and top with zucchini sauce, or put pasta in the bottom of large pasta bowl and top with zucchini sauce. Serve immediately.

MEDITERRANEAN VEGETABLE BLEND

Serves 4
Preparation time: 15 minutes
Cooking time: 15 minutes

R E C I P E   T I P S

The eggplant can be replaced with yellow summer squash or zucchini squash. The Worthington Vegetable Skallops® add a meatlike texture and flavor. Serve as a light dinner with crusty hard bread.

D O - A H E A D   T I P S

The vegetables can be washed and cut in advance, ready to toss in skillet. Place in airtight plastic bags and refrigerate. This dish tastes best served immediately after cooking.

◆

8	Small red potatoes, cleaned with skins
1	Tablespoon olive oil
2	Cups Worthington Vegetable Skallops, cut in strips
1	Green bell pepper, cut in strips
1	Onion, sliced thin and separated into rings
2	Cloves garlic, minced
1	Small eggplant, thinly sliced
1	Teaspoon dried oregano *or* 1 tablespoon fresh oregano leaves, chopped
1	Bay leaf
2	Tablespoons lemon juice
2	Tablespoons fresh chopped parsley *or* 2 teaspoons dried parsley
$\frac{1}{2}$	Teaspoon turmeric
$\frac{1}{2}$	Teaspoon paprika
1	Bunch of chicory *or* romaine lettuce leaves
1	Tomato, sliced, to garnish

❶ In medium-sized saucepan over medium heat, bring potatoes and small amount of water to a boil. Reduce heat to medium-low; cover and cook 10 to 15 minutes or until tender. Drain and cool slightly, slice into quarters and set aside.

❷ Meanwhile, heat oil in large skillet over medium heat, sauté Vegetable Skallops strips, bell pepper, onion, and garlic until scallops are lightly browned and pepper and onion are tender. Stir in eggplant, oregano, and bay leaf. Cook 5 to 10 minutes, or until vegetables are tender-crisp, stirring often. Remove bay leaf and stir in lemon juice. Add cooked potatoes, parsley, turmeric, and paprika; toss gently. Serve over a bed of chicory or romaine lettuce leaves. Garnish with fresh tomatoes and parsley.

GRILLED POTATOES AND VEGETABLES WITH ROASTED GARLIC AND BASIL

Serves 4

Preparation time: 15 minutes
Cooking time: 20 minutes

M E N U   T I P S

This wonderful grilled vegetable feast is a whole meal. Even the bread comes off the grill. The hot grilled vegetables are served on a bed of greens and garnished with fresh tomatoes and basil.

D O - A H E A D   T I P S

The vegetables can be prepared several hours before serving and refrigerated in sealed plastic bags until grilling time. The grilled vegetables taste best hot off the grill, combined with the cool tomatoes and spinach leaves.

◆

Grilled Potatoes:

6	Red potatoes, cut into $\frac{1}{4}$-inch-thick slices
2	Tablespoons extra-virgin olive oil
	Garlic powder, to taste
	Salt to taste (optional)
1	Teaspoon lemon juice

Grilled Vegetables:

2	Tablespoons extra-virgin olive oil
1	Entire garlic bulb
1	Red onion, peeled and thickly sliced
1	Medium *or* 2 small eggplants
2	Zucchini, cut in half lengthwise
1	Yellow pepper, seeded and quartered
1	Red pepper, seeded and quartered
1	Loaf of crusty bread
1	Tomato
3	Large ripe tomatoes (enough for 12 slices)
16	Fresh basil leaves
1	Bunch of spinach leaves

Preparation of grilled potatoes:

❶ Heat grill. Brush potato slices lightly with oil and sprinkle with garlic powder and salt to taste (optional). Place on medium-hot grill and cook, covered, 3 to 5 minutes on each side, or until tender. Drizzle potato slices with small amount of lemon juice and additional garlic powder, to taste.

Preparation of grilled vegetables:

❶ Cut top off the garlic bulb and remove outside cloves. Brush garlic bulb and onion slices lightly with olive oil and place near the edge of a medium-hot grill to cook slowly. Grill for 5 to 10 minutes, turning garlic often. Leave garlic and onions on the grill while cooking the remaining vegetables.

❷ Cut eggplant into thick slices or lengthwise, depending on size of eggplant. Brush eggplant, zucchini halves, yellow squash, and peppers lightly with oil and place in center of grill. Cook a few minutes per side, turning once, until vegetables are seared and brown.

❸ Slice bread and brush with oil. Grill on both sides until brown. Cut tomato in half and rub over one side of hot bread; discard tomato.

❹ To assemble: On large platter lined with spinach leaves, arrange grilled potato slices, grilled vegetables, bread, onions, and garlic. Place cold tomato slices on platter and tuck basil leaves in between tomato slices. With a small knife remove the softened garlic from cloves and spread on toasted bread, potato slices, and vegetables for the delicious taste of roasted garlic.

Why should vegetarians miss out on the fun of outdoor grilling? Move over, hamburgers, and make room for something better.

LINGUINE VEGETABLE TOSS

Serves 6-8

Preparation time: 20 minutes
Cooking time: 15 minutes

M E N U   T I P S

This is a whole meal in one dish. Add a tossed green salad and crusty bread to complete the picture. To vary the recipe, add small broccoli pieces to the vegetable sauté, or add 2 to 4 additional cups of crushed canned tomatoes to the sautéed mixture. This makes the sauté more like a sauce. Use any shape of pasta you like. Make sure that the pasta has JUST been rinsed in water and is not sticky before you toss it with the vegetable mixture. Or you can toss the pasta with a little olive oil to prevent it from becoming sticky. This also helps the vegetable mixture coat the pasta evenly.

D O - A H E A D   T I P S

Make this dish a day ahead and refrigerate until serving time.

◆

1	Pound linguine noodles *or* pasta of your choice
2	Cups carrots, peeled and cut into very thin julienne strips
3	Tablespoons light olive oil (*or* $^1/_2$ part oil to $^1/_2$ part water to lower fat)
1	Large onion, chopped
2	Cups mushrooms, sliced *or* chopped
1	Red pepper, sliced in thin strips
8	Large garlic cloves, minced
2	Tablespoons dried oregano *or* 4 tablespoons fresh oregano, chopped
3	Tablespoons dried basil *or* $^1/_2$ cup fresh basil, chopped
2	Cups zucchini, unpeeled and cut in thin julienne strips
8	Scallions, sliced
2	Cups unsalted sundried tomatoes, rehydrated in pasta water and chopped
4	Cups fresh plum tomatoes, chopped in large chunks
1	Teaspoon garlic powder (optional)
	Salt to taste (optional)

❶ In large saucepan, start water for pasta.
Note: A short cut to rehydrate sundried tomatoes: place them in a metal colander and dip the colander into the boiling pasta water before adding the pasta. Keep them in the boiling water for 3 to 5 minutes or until tomatoes are slightly softened; then remove them from the water and drain. Chop tomatoes in large pieces to use in sautéed vegetable mixture.

❷ In large deep skillet over high heat, combine olive oil (if using water to lower fat use $^1/_2$ the olive oil called for, and add the water after you put in the vegetables), onion, mushrooms, red peppers, and fresh garlic. Cook until vegetables are just tender. Add oregano, basil, zucchini, and scallions and continue cooking until zucchini is tender and scallions are wilted. Add rehydrated chopped sundried tomatoes, fresh tomato, garlic powder, and salt to taste. Simmer until tomatoes are heated through. Set aside.

❸ During the last five minutes the sauté is cooking, put pasta and carrots in the boiling water. (The water will be reddish colored from rehydrating the dried tomatoes.) Cook the pasta 5 to 8 minutes or until just tender. (The carrots will also be perfectly done if they have been cut in thin enough julienne strips.) Drain pasta and carrots and put back in the saucepan that they were cooked in.

❹ To assemble: Add a portion of the vegetable sautéed mixture to the pasta and carrots and toss until the pasta is well coated and the vegetables are evenly distributed. Then add the remaining vegetable mixture. The trick is to toss the pasta mixture very well before serving, so the vegetables do not fall to the bottom. Serve immediately in a large pasta serving bowl or on individual plates.

> ❧
> **M**y husband's cousin, Olsa Baker, spent a day with me experimenting with recipes for this book. We had a wonderful time adapting this one.
> ❧

> I tried Mazidra for the first time with our dear friends Alan and Julie Dybdahl in a Lebanese restaurant in Baton Rouge, Lousiana.

MAZIDRA

Serves 5
Total preparation time using precooked lentils and rice:
10 minutes
Preparation time using uncooked lentils and rice:
20 minutes
Cooking time for dried lentils: 30-35 minutes
Baking time for assembled Mazidra: 10 minutes

M E N U   T I P S

Serve the Mazidra with one of the tabouli salads from the salad section. Add hummus and pita bread for an authentic and nutritionally balanced Mediterranean meal. The flavor of sautéed onions and olive oil saturates the layers of lentils to provide a mouthwatering, nutritious legume dish. The rice can be served as a side dish or layered under the lentils and onions.

D O - A H E A D   T I P S

The lentils and the rice can be made ahead of time and warmed just before assembling. Increase the baking time, if necessary, to be sure all ingredients are bubbling-hot.

Lentils:

2	Cups *or* 8 ounces dried lentils
4	Cups water
1	Teaspoon McKay's Chicken-Style Seasoning
3 - 4	Garlic cloves, minced, *or* 2 teaspoons garlic powder
1	Bay leaf, whole
	Salt to taste
$^1/_2$	Cup uncooked whole-grain rice and 2 cups water
or 3	Cups precooked whole-grain rice
3	Large onions, sliced in thin whole rings
4	Tablespoons light olive oil *or* canola oil

❶ Prepare uncooked rice according to the directions on page 10. If using precooked rice, just rewarm it.

❷ In large saucepan, combine dried lentils, water, chicken seasoning, garlic, bay leaf, and salt. Bring to a boil and turn temperature down; cover and simmer for approximately 30 minutes or until lentils are tender. Set aside.

❸ In large skillet, sauté onion rings in olive oil until tender. If you wish, add additional olive oil and water to make a broth.

❹ To assemble: On individual oven-proof serving plates put about one cup of cooked lentils spread thin. Spread generous portion of sautéed onions with onion/olive oil broth on lentils. Bake each plate of lentils in preheated 450° F oven for approximately 10 minutes or until onions begin to brown and the edges of the lentils get slightly crispy. This will marinate the onion mixture through the lentils. Serve immediately with a side dish of rice.

*ile on the gravy! It's oil-free
and full of flavor—the perfect comple-
ment to this Potato Primavera*

POTATO PRIMAVERA

Serves 4

Preparation time: 20 minutes
Microwave baking time: 20 minutes in both microwave & oven
Conventional baking time: 50 minutes

R E C I P E   T I P S

This hearty main dish meal is sure to be a winner with all potato lovers. Just serve with a tossed green salad and fresh baked whole-grain bread to make a balanced meal. Be sure to choose the largest russet baking potatoes, because they are the main course of this meal.

D O - A H E A D   T I P S

You can time-bake the potatoes so they are ready when you get home from work. You can also partially cook them in the microwave and finish baking them in the oven to create a crisp potato. You can wash and cut the fresh vegetables 1 to 2 days ahead and store in sealed containers. If you are using onion it should be stored separately in an airtight bag.

◆

4	Large russet baking potatoes
2	Cups broccoli florets
2	Cups cauliflower florets
2	Cups carrots, sliced diagonally
1	Cup onion, sliced thinly
1	Cup zucchini, slices
2	Cups **Guilt-free Gravy** (recipe following)

❶ Wash and scrub potatoes and prick with a fork. Wrap each potato in tinfoil or spray all sides of potato with Pam and place on baking sheet. Bake at 425° F for 50 minutes.

To speed up preparation, partially microwave potatoes: Prick potatoes with fork. Place on microwave-safe plate and cover with a paper towel. Cook on high power for 20 minutes. Then place on baking sheet and spray with nonstick vegetable spray; put in 425° F oven for 20 minutes to finish baking and give the potatoes a crispy skin.

❷ While potatoes are cooking, wash and prepare vegetables, cutting into bite-sized pieces. Be sure the pieces are large enough to look attractive and hold together when cooked. Wait to steam vegetables until potatoes are 10 minutes from being done and gravy is ready.

❸ Prepare Guilt-free Gravy, using the following recipe.

❹ Steam vegetables until just tender. After adding vegetables to steamer and the water begins to boil, remove the lid for 2 to 3 minutes to release the oxalic acids that turn the green vegetables brown. Then cover and continue steaming until crisp-tender.

❺ To assemble: Cut each baked potato in half. Pour gravy over the potato and top with 2 cups of mixed, steamed vegetables. Cover the steamed vegetables with additional gravy. Remember to be liberal with the gravy because it is the key to this recipe, and it is guilt-free!

GUILT-FREE GRAVY

Serves 4

Makes 5 to 6 cups, depending on consistency desired
Preparation time: 8 minutes
Cooking time: 10 minutes

R E C I P E   T I P S

This basic gravy can be adapted to a variety of flavors. Try adding your favorite seasonings—like Savorex paste, which gives you a beeflike flavor, G. Washington Broth mix in the Onion, Golden, or Beefy Brown flavor, or soy sauce for an Oriental touch. Serve it over potatoes, rice, or vegetarian roasts or patties.

◆

1	Large onion, chopped
2	Cloves garlic, chopped, *or* 1 teaspoon garlic powder
$^1/_2$	Cup blanched slivered almonds (be sure to use almonds without the skins)
1	Cup water
2	Cups water
5	Tablespoons flour
4 - 5	Teaspoons McKay's Chicken-Style Seasoning
2	Teaspoons nutritional yeast flakes (optional)

❶ In large skillet, sauté chopped onion in 1 to 2 tablespoons of water, cover and let onion steam until tender. Add additional water, 1 tablespoon at a time, if needed to keep onion from burning. Add garlic and steam an additional 2 minutes.

❷ In blender, blend almonds with 1 cup water until smooth. Be sure to blend for several minutes and scrape the sides of the blender bowl frequently, to be sure that the almonds are totally smooth, like the consistency of milk. This may take several minutes in some blenders. Add additional water, flour, chicken seasoning, and optional yeast flakes and blend well.

❸ Add blended mixture to sautéed onion and garlic and bring to a boil for approximately 3 minutes, stirring constantly. As gravy thickens you may need to add more water to bring to desired consistency.

NEW RED POTATOES AND VEGETABLE MEDLEY

Serves 4
Preparation time: 15 minutes
Cooking time: 20 minutes

R E C I P E   T I P S

This recipe can be made without dairy products by using Tofu Sour Cream and the optional grated Soy Cheese. Serve this dish with a garden fresh tossed salad and crusty, whole-grain rolls.

D O - A H E A D   T I P S

The potatoes and vegetables can be washed and prepared for steaming. The Tofu Sour Cream can be made ahead and the green onions and chopped tomatoes prepared and stored separately and tossed together before serving.

◆

10	Small red potatoes
2	Cups **Tofu Sour Cream** (recipe in variation section) *or* low-fat sour cream
$^1/_2$	Cup green onions, thinly sliced
$^1/_2$	Cup fresh tomatoes, chopped
1	Cup carrots, thinly sliced diagonally
1	Cup cauliflower, bite-sized florets
1	Cup broccoli, bite-sized florets
1	Cup low-fat soy cheese *or* mozzarella cheese, grated fine (optional)

❶ Scrub potatoes and place on steamer in saucepan and steam until tender, approximately 20 minutes. Cut potatoes in half and keep warm.

To microwave, place potatoes and $^1/_2$ cup of water in microwave-safe baking dish and cook, covered, on high for 10 minutes. Turn dish and bake an additional 5 to 10 minutes or until tender; drain water off potatoes immediately to prevent them from getting soggy. Cut cooked potatoes in half and keep warm.

❷ While potatoes are cooking prepare Tofu Sour Cream if desired. (See recipe in variation section.) Put sour cream of choice in small mixing bowl and stir in green onions and tomatoes. Chill until needed.

❸ Place steamer and small amount of water in large saucepan; add carrots and steam for 3 minutes, then add cauliflower and broccoli and steam an additional 5 to 8 minutes or until vegetables are crisp-tender. Remove the lid for 1 to 2 minutes once the water comes back to a boil after adding any green vegetables to preserve the green color. Remove lid and drain water immediately.

To microwave vegetables:
Put $^1/_2$ cup water in covered microwave dish. Add carrots, cauliflower, and broccoli and cook on high for approximately 8 minutes or until crisp-tender; drain.

To assemble:
Coat 8" x 8" square casserole with nonstick vegetable spray and arrange potato halves in bottom, cut side up. Pierce cut sides of potatoes with fork. Pour sour cream mixture over potato halves and spread evenly. Top with steamed vegetables and sprinkle with the grated soy or low-fat cheese of choice. Be sure to assemble when potatoes and vegetables are still hot and sour cream mixture is cold.

Everyone loves the light, refreshing taste of new potatoes. This recipe brings out the best in them.

This mouthwatering, cholesterol-free pizza is a Saturday night favorite at our house.

HERBED FRENCH BREAD PIZZAS

Serves 8
Preparation time: 15 minutes
Cooking time: 15 minutes

M E N U   T I P S

I serve this Herbed French Bread Pizza with popcorn and fruit salad for a light supper. Top the pizza with any of your favorite vegetable toppings. If you want the vegetables to be well cooked, you may need to blanch them ahead of time. The sauce soaks into the bread quite a bit, especially if you choose a softer variety, so if you like lots of sauce, add more.

1	Loaf of French *or* Italian bread
2	Tablespoons olive oil (optional)
4 - 6	Cups spaghetti sauce
1	Teaspoon garlic powder
1 - 2	Teaspoons dried basil
1 - 2	Teaspoons dried oregano
1	Cup black olives, sliced
1	Cup onions, chopped
1	Cup green peppers, chopped
2	Cups carrots, grated fine
2	Large tomatoes, sliced

❶ Slice bread in half lengthwise. Drizzle both halves with olive oil. Put cut sides together and squeeze lightly to spread olive oil on both sides of bread. This step is optional, but it prevents the bread from soaking up quite as much sauce. Be sure to add additional sauce if you delete this step. Open halves and place cut side up on baking sheet.

❷ In microwave-proof small bowl, place onions and green peppers with a few tablespoons of water, cover and cook on high for 5 minutes or until onions and peppers are crisp-tender. Drain water and cool. This is a optional step if you like your onions and green peppers well done.

❸ On each half begin layering, starting with tomato sauce. Sprinkle with garlic powder, basil, and oregano. Top with black olives, sautéed onions and green peppers. Sprinkle the grated carrots generously and evenly over the top of both halves for a delicious and nutritious replacement to cheddar cheese. Note: Make sure the carrots are finely grated. Very finely grated carrots will cook quickly and be soft—resembling melted cheese.

❹ Bake in 450° F oven for 12 to 15 minutes or until bubbly and bread is lightly browned. Do not let carrots brown. (If the carrots begin to dry out too much while baking, I press them down a little with a spatula so they get remoistened with the sauce underneath.) Top hot pizzas with fresh slices of tomatoes. Cut each half in diagonal slices and serve warm.

BLACK BEANS WITH RICE

Serves 6-8
Preparation time: 15 minutes
Canned black beans and precooked rice
Cooking time: 30 minutes
Dried beans
Cooking time: 2 ¹/₂ hours
Soaking time for dried beans: **Overnight**

R E C I P E   T I P S
This dish is a Caribbean favorite. Add some tortilla chips or crispy corn tortillas on the side and enjoy this hearty meal.

D O - A H E A D   T I P S
If you use dried black beans, they must be soaked overnight before cooking. The rice can be cooked in a heavy pot or rice cooker while the beans are cooking.

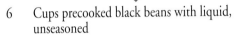

6	Cups precooked black beans with liquid, unseasoned
or 1¹/₂	Cups dried black beans and 8 cups cold water
1¹/₂	Cups dried rice
2	Teaspoons McKay's Chicken-Style Seasoning
2	Teaspoons cumin
3 - 4	Garlic cloves, minced *or* 2 teaspoon garlic powder
2	Bay leaves
2	Teaspoons dried oregano
1	Teaspoon salt
1	Medium onion, chopped
1	Green pepper, chopped
2	Tablespoons lemon juice
1	16-ounce can tomatoes, cut up (optional)
1	Cup green peas, blanched
1	Cup tomatoes, chopped
2	Scallions, sliced thin
2	Tablespoons low-fat sour cream (optional) *or* **Tofu Sour Cream** (recipe in variation section) (optional)

Dried bean preparation:

❶ Rinse beans and soak in 6 cups of cold water overnight. (Do not use the quicker method of first boiling and then soaking beans for only 1 hour. This causes black beans to lose their skins.) Drain water and rinse beans.

❷ Combine the soaked beans, 8 cups of cold water, McCay's Chicken-Style Seasoning, cumin, garlic, bay leaves, oregano, and salt. Bring to a boil; reduce heat. Simmer, covered for 2 hours. Stir in onion, green pepper, lemon juice, and canned tomatoes. Cook an additional 20 to 30 minutes or until onion and green pepper are tender and beans are done. Discard bay leaves.

Canned bean preparation:

❶ In 4-quart saucepan, combine canned beans, McKay's Chicken-Style Seasoning, cumin, garlic, bay leaves, oregano, salt, onion, green pepper, lemon juice, and canned tomatoes. Bring to a boil; cover and let simmer on medium-low temperature for approximately 30 minutes or until vegetables are tender.

Rice preparation:

Prepare rice following the instructions on page 10.

To assemble:
Ladle a 1- to 2-cup serving of beans into a large soup dish. Spoon ¹/₂ cup rice on top of beans. Sprinkle with green peas, green onions, and fresh chopped tomatoes *or* radishes. Garnish with dollop of low-fat *or* tofu sour cream and serve.

Black beans and rice combine to make a perfectly balanced protein for the vegetarian.

D E S S E R T

PEACHES AND RASPBERRY TOPPER
A perfect encore to a summer meal.

Recipe on page 90

Indulge in desserts that won't weigh you down!

Why is it that whenever we decide to watch our waistlines or make healthier eating choices, desserts are the first things we vow to give up? Well, here is good news. You can have tantalizing desserts that are low in calories and fat and still satisfy your sweet tooth. So treat yourself, and have another bite! Most of us are afflicted with a sweet tooth that craves a little something sweet after a meal. Oh, we know a piece of fresh fruit is naturally sweet, but at times our sweet tooth wants more. It wants rich. It wants creamy!

Give these desserts a try, and satisfy your sweet tooth. They are a snap to make and so light in calories and cholesterol that you won't need to feel even slightly guilty.

Never deprive yourself of desserts again!

These wonderful recipes are doable and delicious, especially when you take advantage of the variety of fresh fruits available in season in the produce department of your supermarket, or at your local farmer's market. The nondairy, no-cholesterol fruit sauces and purees included can bring limitless variety to your dessert repertoire.

Do take the time to make dessert—you'll find these recipes will fit into the tightest time schedule. But don't overdo. Even the skinniest dessert can be disastrous when you eat the entire bowlful!

Try the variety of fresh fruit combinations with fruit-sweetened sauces and cholesterol-free, nondairy whipped topping served on platters or as parfaits. Sip the cool, refreshing fruit smoothie or experiment with the frozen fruit bars in an assortment of flavors. Check out the **Peanut Butter Fingers** and the **Granola Bars**— baked desserts that are easily prepared and have a short baking time.

Then move on to the fruit-sweetened pies. They require a bit more preparation and baking time, but I included them for those special occasions when you want to serve a traditional pie in a lower calorie, fruit-sweetened, mouthwatering package. These recipes will convince your family and friends that healthy doesn't have to mean giving up those goodies your sweet tooth craves.

PEACHES WITH CREAMY RASPBERRY TOPPER

Serves 2
Preparation time: 5 minutes

R E C I P E   T I P S

Try this raspberry topper over a variety of seasonal fresh fruits, such as mangoes in the summer or pears in the fall. For a larger group, this dish can be made in a pie plate. Put a layer of peaches on the bottom, top with the creamy raspberry topper, garnish, and serve.

D O - A H E A D   T I P S

The nondairy cream can be made ahead and chilled until serving.

◆

4	Ounces low-fat flavored yogurt, vanilla, lemon, *or* pineapple	
or	$^1/_2$	Cup **Tofu Whipped Cream** (recipe in variation section)
$^1/_4$	Cup fresh *or* loose-packed frozen raspberries	
1	Cup fresh, frozen, *or* canned peaches, sliced	
2	Teaspoons sliced almonds, toasted	
	Fresh raspberries, to garnish	
	Mint sprigs, to garnish	

❶ Combine your choice of yogurt *or* Tofu Whipped Cream and the fresh *or* frozen raspberries in a small bowl. Set aside.

❷ Divide peach slices between two dessert dishes. Spoon half of the yogurt *or* tofu-cream mixture over peaches in each dessert dish. Sprinkle with almonds. If desired, garnish with extra whole raspberries and mint leaves.

Pictured on page 88

Experiment with various glass shapes when you assemble this tasty treat.

PEACHES SUPREME

Serves 6
Preparation time: 10 minutes

R E C I P E   T I P S

Vary this dessert by trying different flavors of pudding. For the nondairy option, change the flavor of the pudding by changing the fruit juice used to sweeten *or* the type of extracts used to flavor. Top with a variety of fruits.

D O - A H E A D   T I P S

The puddings can be made ahead and assembled with fruit just before serving.

◆

Dairy Version:

1	4-serving-size package of reduced-calorie instant vanilla pudding
2	Cups nonfat milk
1	8-ounce carton low-fat vanilla yogurt
2	Cups peaches, nectarines, *or* plums
$^1/_2$	Cup fresh *or* loose-packed frozen blueberries (optional)

Nondairy version:

Tofu vanilla pudding

2	Cups medium-firm tofu, drained and mashed
$^1/_3$- $^1/_2$	Cup unsweetened pineapple juice, *or* fruit juice of choice
2	Tablespoons oil
3	Tablespoons honey *or* sugar
2	Teaspoons vanilla
$^1/_2$	Teaspoon almond extract (optional)
$^1/_4$	Teaspoon salt

❶ Prepare instant pudding according to package directions, using 2 cups nonfat milk. Fold in vanilla yogurt. Spoon the pudding mixture into 6 dessert dishes. Arrange the peach slices on top of the pudding mixture and garnish with blueberries.

Directions for nondairy version:

❷ In bowl, combine tofu vanilla pudding ingredients and mix well, add more juice if needed to sweeten or to thin consistency for blending. In blender container, add half of pudding mixture and blend until smooth. Repeat with other half. Spoon the tofu pudding mixture into 6 dessert dishes and chill until set. Just before serving, arrange the peach slices on top of the pudding mixture and garnish with blueberries.

PEARS IN ORANGE SAUCE

Serves 4
Preparation time: 10 minutes
Cooking time: 10 minutes

D O - A H E A D   T I P S
The orange sauce can be made ahead and warmed to a pourable consistency just before serving.

◆

2	Medium Bartlett pears, nearly ripe but still firm
1	Cup water
$2/_3$	Cup orange juice
2	Tablespoons lemon juice
2	Teaspoons cornstarch
3	Tablespoons sugar *or* honey
$1/_4$	Teaspoon finely shredded orange peel
$1/_4$	Teaspoon salt
	Mint leaves to garnish

❶ Halve pears lengthwise and core. Cut each half into thirds lengthwise, cutting almost through the larger end but leaving connected so that the thin end of the pear can be fanned.

❷ In a 10-inch skillet, bring 1 cup of water to a boil. Add pear halves. Simmer gently, covered, about 10 minutes or until pears are tender. Remove pears from skillet and set aside.

❸ For sauce: In a small saucepan, combine orange juice, lemon juice, and cornstarch. Whisk until the cornstarch is dissolved with no lumps. Add sugar, orange peel, and salt. Cook over medium heat until thickened and bubbly. Cook and stir 2 minutes more.

❹ To serve, fan one pear half on each serving plate. Spoon some of the sauce over the pear. Garnish with mint leaves.

This recipe enhances pears with a delicious orange sauce.

Serve this papaya-laden tropical fruit treat as a refreshing touch at the end of an elegant meal.

TROPICAL FRUIT PLATE WITH PAPAYA SAUCE

Serves 4
Preparation time: 10 minutes

R E C I P E   T I P S
This recipe can also be made in a parfait dish by alternating the layers of fruit, papaya puree, and frozen yogurt or Tofu Whipped Cream.

D O - A H E A D   T I P S
The papaya sauce can be made ahead. The fruit can be prepared and cut ahead of time and chilled until time to assemble. The Tofu Whipped Cream can be made up to 3 days in advance.

◆

2	Ripe papayas, peeled, seeded (*or* apricots *or* peaches)
	Mixture of tropical fruit, sliced, such as fresh pineapple, bananas, kiwi fruit, and mangoes.
1	Cup lowfat frozen vanilla yogurt
or 1	Cup **Tofu Whipped Cream** (recipe in variation section)

❶ Place papayas in blender container. Cover; blend until smooth.

❷ To assemble: spoon papaya puree onto 4 dessert plates. Arrange fruit slices over puree. Serve with $1/_4$-cup scoop of frozen yogurt or top fruit with Tofu Whipped Cream. Garnish with a few pineapple leaves and serve immediately.

*beautiful, refreshing
dessert—this one is sure to please your
eye and soothe your sweet tooth.*

FRUIT MEDLEY WITH APRICOT SAUCE AND CREAM

Serves 4
Preparation time: 10 minutes
Cooking time: 10-15 minutes

R E C I P E   T I P S
This eye-appealing dessert can be served in a variety of ways. Different fruits will change the whole appearance and taste. Try layering fruit, cream, and sauce in a parfait glass for an appealing encore to any meal.

D O - A H E A D   T I P S
The sauce can be prepared and chilled until assembly time. The Tofu Whipped Cream can be prepared up to 3 days in advance and chilled until serving time. The fresh fruit can be washed and cut several hours before assembly.

◆

1 ½	Cups *or* a 12-ounce package dried apricots
1	Cup apple juice concentrate *or* pineapple juice
8	Ounces low-fat plain *or* vanilla yogurt
or 1	Cup **Tofu Whipped Cream** (recipe in variation section)
4	Cups mixed summer fruit, such as peaches, strawberries, kiwi, blackberries, raspberries, blueberries, pineapple wedges, mangoes, etc.
	Fresh mint, for garnish

❶ Prepare apricot sauce: Soak dried apricots in juice overnight or put dried apricots and juice in covered casserole dish and microwave, or cook in saucepan on stove top for 15 minutes; just until apricots are rehydrated and soft. Drain apricots and reserve liquid to use for thinning, if needed. In blender container or food processor bowl, puree apricots until smooth. Add reserved liquid to thin apricot puree to desired consistency. Chill until serving time.

❷ Yogurt cream: Put cheesecloth or thick paper towel in a sieve. Pour yogurt into the sieve and let stand in the refrigerator for 20 minutes—or longer if you have the time. The longer the yogurt stands, the thicker and creamier it will become. Chill until serving.

Nondairy option:
Prepare Tofu Whipped Cream from the recipe in the variation section. Chill until serving time.

❸ Wash and cut the fruit into serving-sized pieces.

❹ **To assemble:** Arrange fruit on individual serving plates around a ½-cup scoop of drained yogurt cream *or* Tofu Whipped Cream. Pour the apricot sauce over fruit and cream. If the apricot sauce is too thick to pour, add more juice or warm the sauce in the microwave slightly just before pouring.

STRAWBERRY AND CREAM PARFAIT

Serves 4
Preparation time: 15 minutes

R E C I P E   T I P S

This parfait can be made with a variety of fruits and yogurt flavors. The Tofu Whipped Cream or whipped topping of your choice can be flavored with almond extract or finely grated lemon or orange rind. For a dinner party, this dessert can be arranged in a large glass bowl in layers like an English trifle.

D O - A H E A D   T I P S

The strawberry sauce and Tofu Whipped Cream can be prepared ahead of time and chilled. The fruit can also be prepared ahead of time.

◆

1	Cup sliced fresh strawberries
1/4	Cup orange juice
1	Tablespoon sugar (optional)
1	Cup **Tofu Whipped Cream** (recipe in variation section) *or* low-fat vanilla yogurt
1	Large banana, sliced
1	Cup fresh strawberries, sliced (optional)
1	Cup fresh pineapple cubes *or* 1 8-ounce can pineapple chunks, drained
1	Cup fresh blueberries
1/4	Cup sliced almonds to garnish

❶ In blender container or food processor bowl with metal chop blade, combine strawberries, juice, and optional sugar; blend until smooth.

❷ Prepare Tofu Whipped Cream according to directions in the variation section or use the vanilla yogurt.

❸ To assemble: In 4 parfait glasses, layer fruit, cream *or* yogurt, and strawberry sauce. Repeat layers, ending with strawberry sauce. Garnish with sliced almonds.

Strawberry lovers will delight in this simple, sinless dessert.

Try this for a light and refreshing dessert at the end of a hearty meal.

APRICOT WHIP

Makes 7 half-cup servings
Preparation time: 10 minutes
Cooking time: 10 minutes

R E C I P E   T I P S

This Apricot Whip can be served over fruit, used as a topping in fruit parfaits, or poured into a pie shell and garnished with fresh fruit for a delicious tart.

D O - A H E A D   T I P S

May be made the day before serving and chilled.

◆

20	Dried apricot halves (about 1 cup)
1	Cup apple juice concentrate *or* pineapple juice
6	Dates, chopped (optional), for sweetening
2	Cups firm tofu
1/4	Cup honey *or* sugar
1	Teaspoon vanilla
1/8	Teaspoon salt
2	Tablespoons oil

❶ In saucepan, combine apricot halves, apple juice concentrate, and optional dates. Simmer over medium heat until apricots are softened. Transfer mixture to blender container and blend until smooth and creamy.

❷ Add tofu, honey *or* sugar, salt, and oil to the apricot puree mixture and continue blending until smooth. Pour into individual serving dishes. Chill until set.

❸ Just before serving, garnish with fresh fruit *or* nuts.

FROZEN FRUIT BARS

Makes 16 to 18 bars
Preparation time: 10 minutes
Freezing time: 4-6 hours

R E C I P E   T I P S

Making these bars may sound unreasonable for those of you who barely have time to get dinner on the table, until you consider that they require only a few minutes of your time. The freezer does the work. This recipe has endless variation possibilities in addition to those listed. Make a lot—these treats disappear fast!

D O - A H E A D   T I P S

These bars must be made at least 6 hours before serving time. You'll need plastic popsicle molds or small paper cups and wooden sticks. Plastic spoons can be substituted for the sticks.

◆

Strawberry Supreme Bars

1 1/4	Cups fresh *or* loose-packed frozen strawberries
1 1/2	Cups tofu milk, soy milk, *or* low-fat dairy milk
1	Small banana, cut into chunks
1/4	Teaspoon vanilla extract

Orange-Raspberry Fruit Bars

1	12-ounce can frozen orange juice concentrate
1	Cup fresh *or* loose-packed frozen raspberries
3	Cups soy milk, tofu milk, *or* low-fat dairy milk
1/4	Teaspoon vanilla extract

Peaches and Cream Bars

3	Cups tofu milk, soy milk, *or* low-fat dairy milk
1	16-ounce can sliced peaches packed in juice (do not drain)
1	Small banana, cut into chunks
1/2	Teaspoon almond extract

Piña Colada Bars

2	Cups unsweetened pineapple juice
1	Medium banana, cut in chunks
1	Cup fresh *or* loose-packed frozen strawberries
1	Cup tofu milk, soy milk, *or* low-fat dairy milk
1/2	Teaspoon coconut extract

Directions for all bars:

❶ Chill all ingredients thoroughly. Place in a blender or food processor and blend until smooth and well combined. Depending on the time available, your preferences and the supplies and equipment you have on hand, continue with the method of your choice.

❷ **Method 1:**
Pour blended mixture into a shallow pan and freeze until somewhat frozen but not rock hard. With an ice cream scoop, scoop chunks of the frozen mixture into a blender or food processor with chop blade and process until smooth. Quickly spoon the mixture into popsicle molds or small paper cups.

Method 2:
Pour blended mixture into a small ice-cream maker holding about 5 cups. Following manufacturer's directions, freeze mixture until it is somewhat frozen but still soft. Spoon into popsicle molds or small paper cups.

Method 3:
If you are really pressed for time, pour the unfrozen mixture from the food processor or blender right into the popsicle molds or small paper cups. (The finished product will be harder than with other methods.)

❸ When spooning mixture into molds, press down to remove air pockets and leave 1/8" to 1/4" of space at the top of molds. Place a wooden or plastic stick in the center of each treat. (If preparing these treats for children, consider their ages and choose a stick that is appropriately safe. Wrapped-paper sucker safety sticks, designed especially for small children, may be purchased at candy-makers' supply stores.) Freeze several hours. At serving time, run hot water over the mold to dislodge the treat. If you have extra mixture left and no more molds, place in container and return to freezer. Eat like ice cream before it gets too hard.

These delicious and healthy frozen treats will put everyone in a good humor!

PEANUT BUTTER FINGERS

Serves 15
Preparation time: 15 minutes
Baking time: 12 minutes

R E C I P E   T I P S

These treats are hard to resist! Vary the recipe by using crunchy peanut butter in the cookie crust, or by mixing carob chips into the cookie crust before baking. You can still add a layer of melted carob chips.

D O - A H E A D   T I P S

These treats can be frozen in an airtight container lined with waxed paper and with waxed paper between the layers of cookies. They taste delicious frozen or at room temperature.

◆

$3/4$	Cup peanut butter, smooth *or* crunchy
$1/3 - 1/2$	Cup honey, to desired sweetness
$1/2$	Teaspoon vanilla
1	Cup finely ground whole-wheat flour
1	Cup quick-cooking oats
$1/4$	Teaspoon salt
1	Cup sweetened carob chips

Peanut Butter Icing:

$1/4$	Cup smooth peanut butter
1	Tablespoon tofu milk powder *or* powdered milk
1	Tablespoon cornstarch
1 - 2	Tablespoons honey
$1/4$	Teaspoon vanilla
1 - 2	Teaspoons water to thin icing to spreadable consistency

❶ Cream together peanut butter, honey, and vanilla. Add salt and flour and mix. Add oats last and mix well. Spray 9" x 13" baking pan with nonstick vegetable spray. Spread peanut butter mixture evenly in pan and bake at 350° F for approximately 12 minutes, watching closely to prevent overbrowning.

❷ Sprinkle carob chips evenly over hot cookie crust. Let chips stand until they are melted. (Make sure carob chips are at room temperature, or they won't melt.) When chips have melted, spread them evenly over cookie layer with spatula. If the carob chips do not melt after a few minutes, begin spreading them with a moistened spatula, continuing to moisten spatula as needed. Set aside to cool.

❸ Prepare peanut butter icing by placing all ingredients in small bowl and mixing well. Spread over the cooled carob layer. Cut in small squares and serve warm or at room temperature.

Peanut butter and chocolate lovers, watch out, you are in for a sweet-tooth treat! My friend Trish Hayden shared these appetizing treats with me. They have been a regular feature at our house ever since.

BANANA MANGO SMOOTHIE

Serves 4
Makes 4 $1/2$ cups
Preparation time: 5-10 minutes

R E C I P E   T I P S

This dessert is high in vitamin A and full of flavor. Try adding other fruits to add variety to this smoothie.

D O - A H E A D   T I P S

This smoothie can be made the day before and chilled until serving time.

◆

1	Cup ripe mangoes, chopped
1	Cup fresh pineapple chunks
1	Medium banana, cut into fourths
2	Cups low-fat vanilla yogurt
or 2	Cups **Tofu Whipped Cream** (recipe in variation section)
2	Tablespoons honey
1	Teaspoon lime juice
$1/2$	Teaspoon vanilla extract

❶ In blender container, combine all ingredients and process until smooth. Chill thoroughly and serve in tall glasses garnished with pineapple wedges and mango chunks, skewered on toothpicks.

GRANOLA FRUIT BARS

Serves 15
Preparation time: 10 minutes
Baking time: 30 minutes

RECIPE TIPS

There are many ways to vary the filling in this recipe. The jam version forms a bar that you can pick up and eat. You can also use rehydrated dried fruit (dried apricots, dates, figs, etc.) blended with apple juice or pineapple juice to make a thick puree as a filling. The fresh-fruit version makes a fruit crisp dessert that is served up with a spatula, placed on individual plates, and eaten with a fork. Try topping it with Tofu Whipped Cream or the whipped topping of your choice.

DO-AHEAD TIPS

These bars freeze well in an airtight container layered with wax paper. You'll want to keep a supply on hand for last-minute after-meal sweet-tooth cravings.

◆

$^1/_3$	Cup oil
$^1/_2$	Cup honey
1	Cup nuts, chopped (almonds, pecans, etc.)
1	Cup whole-wheat *or* white flour
2	Cups quick-cooking oats
16	Ounces sugarless fruit-sweetened jam (raspberry, apricot, *or* blueberry)
or 3	Cups sliced fresh *or* canned peaches, drained; fresh *or* loose-packed frozen blueberries, *or* apples that have been sliced and sprinkled with cinnamon and lemon juice.

❶ Cream together oil and honey. Mix in nuts, flour, and oats.

❷ Spray nonstick vegetable spray in 9" x 13" baking dish. Pour in $^1/_2$ of crumb mixture and lightly flatten. Spread jam *or* fresh fruit of choice over crumb crust. Top with remaining crumb mixture and press down lightly. Bake at 350° F for 30 minutes. Cut into squares and serve warm or at room temperature.

BOWL-CRUST APPLE PIE

Serves 8
Preparation time: 25 minutes
Cooking time: 5 minutes
Baking time: 45 minutes

RECIPE TIPS

This uniquely shaped, bottom-crust-only pie is filled with apples that are tossed in a sugar-free fruit sauce and baked to perfection. Top with creamy Tofu Whipped Cream or the whipped topping of your choice for a dessert feast. This crust can also be filled with other combinations of fruit. Just replace the apples with peaches, plums, etc., and use the same fruit sweetened sauce.

DO-AHEAD TIPS

When making piecrust, make a few extra at the same time. Roll out each crust and place waxed paper on top. Turn crust over and place waxed paper on the other side as well. Fold in quarters, seal in a plastic bag, and freeze for later use.

◆

	Pastry for one crust (see recipe in this section)
1	12-ounce can frozen apple juice concentrate, thawed and undiluted
2	Tablespoons cornstarch
1	Tablespoon margarine
1	Teaspoon ground cinnamon *or* coriander
1	Teaspoon vanilla extract
1	Teaspoon lemon juice
6	Medium-sized tart cooking apples (McIntosh, Cortland, *or* Granny Smith), peeled, cored, and cut into thin wedges.

❶ Make pastry. Roll out into a 14" to 16" circle. Place in 10-inch pie plate, leaving edges uncut. Pastry should extend about 3-inch to 4-inch beyond edges of pie plate. Chill for 20 minutes while preparing filling.

❷ In medium-sized saucepan, combine cold apple juice concentrate and cornstarch. Whisk until all the cornstarch is dissolved and no lumps remain. Place over medium heat and cook until thickened and bubbly. Stir in margarine, cinnamon, vanilla, and lemon juice. Add apple slices; toss well to coat.

❸ Fill the crust with the apple mixture. Fold the pastry edges up over the apples to form "bowl."

❹ Bake for 45 minutes in a preheated 375° F oven until the apple filling is bubbly and the crust is golden. Cool slightly. Slide the pie out of the pie plate and onto a serving plate or board. Serve with a bowl of Tofu Whipped Cream *or* whipped topping of your choice.

*ore beautiful and fresher-
tasting than the usual cooked fruit pie,
this version makes the most of the delec-
table taste of fresh blueberries.*

BLUEBERRY TART

Serves 8
Preparation time: 20 minutes
Cooking time: 15 minutes
Baking time for piecrust: 10 minutes

R E C I P E   T I P S

Try this tart for a special-occasion dinner on a summer day when fresh blueberries are at their peak. Also try this recipe with fresh strawberries, peaches, blackberries, etc. Taste to adjust sweetener to your preference. The blackberries may need additional sweetener.

D O - A H E A D   T I P S

This tart can be made the day before and chilled until serving time.

◆

	Pastry for one-crust pie
4	Cups fresh blueberries
2	Cups frozen apple juice concentrate, undiluted
1	Cup fresh blueberries
$^1/_2$	Cup water
$^1/_4$	Cup quick-cooking tapioca
1 $^1/_2$	Teaspoons vanilla extract
2	Teaspoons lemon juice

❶ Prepare piecrust using one of the recipes that follow. Roll out and place in bottom of tart pan. Prick dough all over with a fork and bake according to recipe directions.

❷ Prepare blueberry filling: Wash and drain fresh blueberries. In blender container, blend 1 cup of fresh blueberries with apple juice concentrate. Transfer juice mixture to saucepan. Add water and tapioca. Bring to a boil; remove from heat and let stand 5 minutes. Return to heat and bring to a boil again; simmer approximately 5 to 10 minutes, stirring constantly, until tapioca is clear. Stir in vanilla and lemon juice. Let cool slightly (5 to 10 minutes). Toss fresh blueberries into thickened sauce to coat blueberries well; cool.

❷ Pour into baked tart shell and refrigerate 2 to 4 hours or until firmly set before serving. Serve with Tofu Whipped Cream *or* whipped topping of your choice dolloped on each serving or mounded in the center of the tart.

PASTRY CRUST

Makes 1 crust
Preparation time: 5 minutes

R E C I P E   T I P S
This recipe breaks the rules of what it takes to make a light and flaky crust, but I promise you it is light, flaky, easy to make and healthful.

D O - A H E A D   T I P S
This crust can be made ahead, rolled out between waxed paper, folded in quarters, placed in a sealed plastic bag, and frozen until needed.

◆

1 $\frac{1}{4}$ Cups white flour
$\frac{1}{4}$ Teaspoon salt
$\frac{1}{3}$ Cup vegetable oil
4   Tablespoons cold water

❶ Sift flour and salt. Whisk cold water into oil until emulsified. Pour oil mixture into dry mixture. Stir quickly with fork until flour is coated with oil mixture. Be careful not to handle pastry dough too much to prevent a tough crust.

❷ Roll out pastry dough between 2 pieces of waxed paper until it is 2 inches bigger in diameter than the pan you are using. Peel off the top piece of waxed paper and turn rolled pastry over on top of pie or tart pan. Remove waxed paper and fit crust into the pan, removing all air bubbles. Finish the edge according to your preference. If using a tart pan, use your fingers to seal the top edge of crust tightly to the pan to keep it from falling in when you bake it. If you are baking the crust without a filling, be sure to prick the bottom of the pie plate with a fork in several places to prevent the crust from bubbling up. Bake at 375°F for 12-15 minutes.
Options:
Decrease flour by 2 tablespoons and replace with toasted wheat germ. This works well when using the crust for a main dish recipe. If baking the crust without filling, decrease the oil by 1 tablespoon.

This is my friend Wendy Bergman's recipe. Wendy joined us on this book's photo shoot, and made the crust for the blueberry tart shown in the photograph.

MOM'S BLACKBERRY PIE

Serves 8
Preparation time: 20 minutes
Cooking time: 15 minutes
Baking time:

R E C I P E   T I P S
If you have nice sweet blackberries, this fruit-sweetened sauce seasons them just right. If your berries are really tart, you may need to add additional sweetener.

D O - A H E A D   T I P S
Make the crust ahead of time and freeze.

◆

Pastry for two-crust pie
2   Cups frozen apple juice concentrate
$\frac{1}{2}$ Cup water
$\frac{1}{4}$ Cup quick-cooking tapioca
1 $\frac{1}{2}$ Teaspoons vanilla extract
1   Teaspoon almond extract
2   Teaspoons lemon juice
4   Cups of fresh *or* frozen blackberries *or* berries of your choice

❶ Prepare pastry and roll out into two 12-inch circles. Place one crust in pie plate and form to the bottom of the pan. Leave edges untrimmed until top crust is added. Chill crust while making the filling.

❷ In saucepan, combine cold apple juice concentrate, water, and tapioca. Bring to a boil and remove from heat for approximately 5 minutes. Return to a boil and simmer, stirring constantly, for 10 minutes or until tapioca granules are clear and soft. Stir in vanilla, almond extract, and lemon juice and mix well. Taste and add additional sweetener if desired. Add fresh blackberries and toss gently to coat evenly with the tapioca sauce.

❸ Pour mixture into unbaked crust. Top with remaining crust. Trim edges of both crusts, allowing them to extend about one inch beyond edge of pie plate. Seal and flute edges. Cut slits in the top crust to release steam when baking.

❹ Bake at 425° F for 35 to 45 minutes or until crust is nicely browned and juice bubbles through slits. Serve warm with Tofu Whipped Cream topping or lowfat yogurt.

My husband loves blackberry pie. His mother makes it for him every time we visit. This is a fruit-sweetened version of Mom's delicious recipe.

Berries add an eye and tastebud-tempting twist to this low-calorie dessert.

APPLE-BERRY CRISP

Serves 8
Preparation time: 15 minutes
Cooking time: 10 minutes
Baking time: 35 to 45 minutes

RECIPE TIPS
Other fruits also work well in this recipe. Peaches and blueberries make a nice combination.

DO-AHEAD TIPS
The recipe tastes best freshly prepared and straight out of the oven, but if necessary, it can be assembled, baked the day before, and reheated in the oven.

1	12-ounce can frozen apple juice concentrate, undiluted
2	Tablespoons cornstarch
10	Tart cooking apples (McIntosh, Cortland, *or* Granny Smith), peeled, cored, and cut in thin wedges
2	Tablespoons margarine
1	Teaspoon lemon juice
1	Teaspoon cinnamon
2	Cups fresh *or* loose-packed frozen raspberries *or* blackberries

Crumb Topping:

$^1/_3$	Cup vegetable oil
$^1/_3$	Cup honey
$^1/_2$	Cup nuts, chopped
$^1/_2$	Cup flour
2	Cups quick-cooking oats

① In large saucepan or skillet, combine cold apple juice concentrate and cornstarch. Whisk cornstarch until it is completely dissolved and no lumps remain. Cook over medium heat until thickened. Add margarine, lemon juice, and cinnamon. Stir to blend all ingredients together. Remove mixture from heat, pour over sliced apples and toss well.

② Prepare crumb topping: In mixing bowl cream together oil and honey. Add chopped nuts, flour, and oats. Toss well, coating all dry ingredients with the oil-and-honey mixture.

③ In 9" x 13" baking dish sprayed with nonstick spray, place the apple filling. Add the berries, distributing in an even layer over the apples. Sprinkle crumb topping evenly over the fruit. Bake at 350° for 30 to 40 minutes or until crumb topping is toasted golden brown and filling is bubbling. Serve warm with Tofu Whipped Cream topping or whipped topping of your choice.

BREAD

Crusty, warm, fragrant—no
wonder they call it
"the staff of life!"

The Art of Making Homemade, Whole-grain Bread!

When I was a girl, there was nothing I loved better than the aroma of fresh-baked bread filling the house. Grandma Thomas, my Dad's mother, taught my mom all the tricks to making great homemade bread. Mom became the best bread maker around, and later I became her biggest fan and most avid bread making student.

Whole-grain bread is one of the best foods you can eat. Contrary to what many people think, bread is not fattening. The three pats of butter or two heaping spoonfuls of mayonnaise you put on it are the problem. Good whole-grain bread is so flavorful you can leave off those high-fat toppings and hardly notice that they are gone.

Whole-grain bread becomes the main course in the meatless diet. Bread that is made with a variety of whole grains can be a satisfying meal, almost by itself. With fresh 100 percent whole-grain breads in your diet, you'll be sure to get enough servings from the grains group, the foundation of the "Eating Right Pyramid."

Bread is the best fast food you can find. It takes me about an hour and a half to make a week's worth of homemade bread for my family of four. McDonald's may not even tempt your kids when homemade bread is around.

If you're a busy person but you'd like to start making bread for your family, a bread-making machine might be the answer for you. There are two types of bread machines: kitchen machines that mix and knead the dough until it is ready to be put into pans, and auto-bakers, which do the whole process of kneading and baking.

My choice of kitchen machines is the Magic Mill DLX Kitchen Machine, which kneads 15 pounds of dough at a time. Many people like the Bosch Kitchen Machine, another excellent bread making appliance. I also use a Magic Mill grain mill for milling wheat berries and other grains and legumes into flour. (See Pantry Section for purchasing information.)

Auto-bake machines mix the ingredients for one loaf, knead the dough, allow it to rise, and bake it. If you buy one of these machines, be sure to get one that has a whole wheat cycle.

If you're new to bread making, read the following basic guide, filled with helpful tips for beginners. This is a formula for one loaf of whole-wheat bread. Use this basic guide, and you can vary the types of bread you make almost endlessly, without worrying about the outcome. Study this formula to learn what goes into a loaf of bread, and why. Following that is a recipe that makes four large loaves, with directions for using a kitchen machine, or making the bread entirely by hand. Also included is one of my favorite auto-bake recipes.

Start a tradition in your house: fill the kitchen with the wonderful aroma of homemade bread!

BASIC BREAD-MAKING FORMULA AND GUIDE

Makes 1 loaf

1	Cup liquid
0 - 4	Tablespoons oil, shortening, *or* melted margarine
1 - 4	Tablespoons sugar
$1/2$-1	Teaspoon salt
1	Tablespoon yeast, active *or* rapid rise
$1/2$-1	Tablespoon gluten flour (optional)
2 $1/2$-3	Cups flour

Liquid:
Vary the liquid with reserved juice from cooked potatoes or vegetables. The basic formula for liquid is as follows: Use 1 cup of liquid for every medium-sized loaf. Be sure that the temperature of the liquid is just slightly warmer than your body temperature.

Yeast:
Dry active yeast or rapid-rising dry yeast is usually used for bread making. The only difference between them is the number of times they need to rise and the speed at which they work. Rapid-rising yeast needs only one rising time and rises 50 percent faster. When you use it, the bread dough can be put directly into loaf pans after kneading, and then allowed to rise. The basic formula for yeast is as follows: Use 1 to 3 level tablespoons of yeast (1 to 3 packets) per 4 cups of liquid. My choice is Red Star's Rapid Rise Yeast. Yeast must be fresh. Check expiration dates before purchasing, and store, tightly sealed, in the refrigerator or freezer. Bring it to room temperature before using. Be sure to use the yeast when it is still foaming.

Sugars:
Honey, molasses, or applesauce in equal portions can be substituted for sugar. Special dietary breads can be made without sugar. A small amount of sugar, however, gives a more tender crust and crumb and aids in browning. Breads of average texture have 1 to 2 tablespoons of sugar per cup of liquid, and sweet dough breads contain 3 to 4 tablespoons per cup.

Fat:
Many hearth breads (breads baked on a baking sheet), such as French bread, have no added fat. They develop a hard crust and a soft center. The average pan-baked loaf contains 1 to 2 tablespoons of fat per cup of liquid in recipe (vegetable oil is recommended). Rich doughs contain 3 to 4 tablespoons of fat for each cup of liquid and are used for specialty breads.

Salt:
The basic formula for salt is $2/3$ to 1 teaspoon of salt per cup of liquid used in recipe.

Magic Mill Dough Enhancer or gluten flour:
This is optional, but helpful in producing a lighter bread for those who do not mill their own flour and use purchased flour.

Whole-wheat flour:
Use no less than 3 and no more than 4 cups of flour per 1 cup of liquid. Use no more than 20 percent other flours or dry ingredients as substitutes for whole-wheat flour, and no more than 2 tablespoons per cup of most other additions. Try adding any of the following dry ingredients to vary your bread: soy, rye, oat, or rice flour; rolled oats; wheat germ; and sprouted grains or seeds. You may also add cooked grains or legumes, such as oatmeal, millet, cornmeal mush, or lentils. Mashed, starchy vegetables, such as potatoes, in very small amounts may also be added. Beginning bread makers should start with 50 percent whole-wheat and 50 percent white flour, and stay away from a large variety of additional ingredients until their bread making skills are perfected.

This basic formula guarantees success—even for the novice bread maker.

> **I**n just five minutes of prep-
> aration time, you can enjoy
> the great taste of homemade
> whole grain bread.

AUTO-BAKE WHOLE-WHEAT BREAD

Makes 1 large loaf
Preparation time: 5 minutes
Rising and cooking time: 4 hours in average bread machine

RECIPE TIPS
This is a great alternative for homemade bread if you have an auto-bake
machine. If you are shopping for one, be sure the machine you're considering has a whole-wheat setting.

DO-AHEAD TIPS
Set the timer to give you fresh-baked bread when you wake up in the
morning or when you walk in the door in the evening.

2	Tablespoons fruit juice concentrate
$^7/_8$	Cup warm water
1	Teaspoon salt
1	Tablespoon margarine
2	Cups whole-wheat flour
or 1	Cup whole-wheat *and* 1 cup white flour
1	Packet Red Star dry yeast

❶ Mount the kneader blade on the drive shaft in the bread case. Put the ingredients into the bread case in the order listed. Place the bread case in the main unit. (If your auto-baker does not have a setting for whole-grain bread, use 1 cup whole-wheat flour and 1 cup white flour.)

❷ The fruit juice concentrate can be replaced with applesauce, honey, molasses, *or* sugar. If you do this, increase warm water to 1 full cup.

❸ Begin the baking process following machine directions.

❹ After the buzzer sounds remove the bread from the bread case and place the bread on a wire rack to cool, covered.

WHOLE-WHEAT BREAD

Yield: 4 large loaves or 6 medium-sized loaves
Preparation time: 20 minutes
Rising time: 30 minutes
Baking time: 40 - 45 minutes

R E C I P E   T I P S

With this basic recipe the home baker is free to vary the bread almost endlessly. After the dough has been kneaded, it can be formed into a variety of shapes, such as pizza crusts, dinner rolls, or cinnamon buns.

D O - A H E A D   T I P S

Freeze cooled baked bread in airtight plastic bags. Thaw in microwave on defrost or thaw at room temperature for several hours. (To thaw in microwave, leave bread in opened bag. Cover the top of the loaf with a damp paper towel to prevent drying.)

◆

6	Cups warm water
4 $^1/_2$	Tablespoons *or* 4 packages rapid-rise dry yeast
$^3/_4$	Cup applesauce *or* sugar
$^3/_4$	Cup vegetable oil
2	Tablespoons salt
6	Cups freshly milled whole-wheat flour from hard white wheat berries *or* purchased whole-wheat flour
2 - 3	Tablespoons Magic Mill Dough Enhancer *or* gluten flour (optional). This is important if you are making bread by hand or if you are using purchased flour, which usually has a lower gluten content then freshly milled flour.
10 - 12	Additional cups freshly milled *or* purchased whole-wheat flour

Fill your house with the wonderful aroma of fresh-baked bread!

Bread-machine or handmaking method:

❶ In bread-machine bowl or large mixer bowl, combine the warm water, room-temperature rapid-rise yeast, and sweetener. Mix well and allow to sit until yeast is activated—about 5 minutes. Be sure to use the yeast while it is still foaming and before it sinks. If after 7 minutes the yeast is not bubbling and activated, the water may be too cool or the yeast may not be good. See Basic Bread-making Formula for information on purchasing and storing yeast.

❷ Add oil, salt, 6 cups of flour, and optional dough enhancer or gluten flour. Mix on medium speed of bread machine or by hand until all the flour is moistened. This is the stage when a small amount of extra ingredient, such as a few tablespoons of leftover cooked cereal, a little leftover mashed potatoes, or different flour options can be added. Beat 3 minutes with machine on high or 3 to 5 minutes by hand to work gluten well. Let rise for 8 minutes. Mixture should be bubbling and rising significantly.

❸ Add the last 12 - 14 cups of flour
Bread-machine method
With the machine running on low speed, add 5 cups of flour at a time, waiting after each addition for all the flour to be moistened. Add the last 4 to 6 cups one cup at a time, watching for the dough to begin to hold together and pull away from the sides of the bowl. (The kind of bowl you're using makes a difference here. With a stainless steel bowl like the DLX bread machine has, the dough never totally pulls away from the side as it would with a plastic bowl.) Be sure not to add too much flour. The dough should be slightly sticky to touch, but when you pinch off a small amount of dough and roll it into a ball it should no longer be sticky. It should be light and elastic but not stiff. With practice you'll learn how to tell when just enough flour has been added.

Handmaking method:

Add the flour a cup at a time until the dough becomes too stiff to stir. Then turn the dough out onto a floured surface and knead, adding flour just until the dough is elastic, smooth, and easy to handle. Don't add too much flour, or the bread will be heavy and dry. Experience counts here. Hand-made 100 percent whole-wheat bread that is truly light and moist is very difficult for the beginner to make. You'll improve the odds if you use between 25 percent and 50 percent white flour in the final kneading process. After the last addition of flour, you can oil your hands to make the dough easier to handle, and to prevent adding too much flour, so that the dough does not become too stiff and heavy.

❹ Kneading bread dough
Bread-machine method:

Knead on medium-low speed between 8 and 15 minutes. The slower speed stretches the gluten and gives elasticity to the dough, resulting in a lighter loaf of bread.

Handmaking method:

After the last addition of flour, continue to knead for approximately 10 minutes, using a rolling motion, making long, outward, firm pushes with the palm of the hand, rotating the dough often.

❺ Dividing dough into loaf pans:

Remove kneaded dough from bread machine with oiled hands onto oiled counter. Divide dough into 6 large loaves or 8 small loaves. Heavily coat sides and bottoms of bread pans with nonstick spray. Form each section of dough into a ball and roll vigorously to distribute air bubbles. Shape into loaves. Cover loaf pans with a light towel and let rise for 30 minutes in an 80° to 85°degree environment. Make sure the rising place is not too warm. If finished bread has an off-flavor—a too-yeasty taste—it could be because of overheating during the rising. Temperatures above 85 degrees can destroy the yeast. If the rising place is a little cooler than 80 degrees, the dough may take just a little longer to rise. The dough is ready when it has doubled in size and responds slowly to a light finger touch.

❻ Baking:
Bake loaves in preheated oven at 375° F for 10 minutes or until set. Then lower temperature to 350° F to regulate browning, and bake for approximately 30 to 35 additional minutes for a one-pound loaf, or until nicely browned on all sides. Smaller loaves will take less baking time.

❼
Remove bread from pans and place on cooling racks. (The loaf should feel light for its size.) My mom brushes vegetable shortening on the hot bread to moisten the crust. Other methods include spraying the tops of the bread with nonstick spray, or holding the hot bread on its side and quickly passing the top under running hot water. Cover the bread immediately. The water will quickly absorb in steam and the covered crust will be moistened without the addition of oil. Keep loaves covered until cool.

❽
When completely cool, wrap each loaf in an airtight plastic bag. I use 1/2- to 1-gallon twist-top freezer bags. After a few hours the bread can be frozen.

Let the kids help and make memories as well as bread!

DRINKS

CRANBERRY TEA
Fresh cranberries lend their tart and tangy flavor to this delicious hot drink.

Recipe on page 117

Refreshing Thirst Quenchers

Sipping is getting more appealing these days! With bottled waters, numerous fruit drinks and juices, cool herbal iced teas, and a wide assortment of nonalcoholic, carbonated, and noncarbonated beverages available, not to mention flavored hot beverages, there's no excuse to go around thirsty!

Drink in the labels first.

Take a good look at soft drink and fruit juice labels. You may think that a carbonated drink with added fruit juice is offering your family some extra benefits; however, these bubbly beverages are often high in calories and sodium. It's better—and oh, so easy—to make good drinks yourself. All of the cool sparklers, iced teas, and hot drinks that follow are guaranteed to satisfy your thirstiest whim and are sweetened with natural fruit juices.

Vary the beverages you serve your family and friends. Experiment with new combinations of fruit juices. And be creative about the way you serve them. A little ingenuity will ensure that every sip is satisfying.

In the hot summer weather, frosted glasses are a nice touch. If you have extra freezer-proof glassware, store some in the freezer for a special treat for your family or drop-in guests. Just dip the glasses in water and place them in the freezer for a frosted appearance. This also keeps cool drinks cool longer.

For another hot-weather treat, make your own healthful snow cones. If you have an ice crusher or a blender capable of crushing ice, place 5 or 6 ice cubes in the container and blend them until they are crushed. Puree your favorite fresh fruit and spoon puree over crushed ice in a long-stemmed glass.

Serving punch to a large group of family or friends can be a challenge; it's tough to keep it cold without diluting the flavor with ice. One way to solve this problem is to make an ice ring. Pour a quantity of the punch or a complementary juice combination into a ring-shaped Jell-O mold and freeze. Unmold and place the ice ring into the bottom of the punch bowl. Pour the beverage over it. Decorate the ice ring by freezing whole pieces of fresh fruit, edible flowers such as violets or marigolds, or herbs such as mint or lemon balm into it.

When preparing punch in advance for a large group, chill all of the ingredients beforehand. Mix as many batches as you need and pour them into empty glass containers or well-rinsed milk cartons. Refrigerate or freeze until serving time.

No punch bowl in your cupboard? Use a large salad bowl, or for hot drinks, a Dutch oven or Crock-Pot.

RASPBERRY-LIME ICED TEA

Makes 3 $\frac{1}{2}$ quarts   Serves 12
Preparation time: 5 minutes
Steeping time: 2 hours

R E C I P E   T I P S

I like this tea a little tart. You may prefer it sweeter. Adjust the flavor to suit your preferences.

D O - A H E A D   T I P S

Prepare the steeped tea mixture at least 2 hours ahead of serving time. Make it up to 24 hours in advance; any longer than this and the tea gets too strong and requires much more sweetener.

◆

5	Cups boiling water
2	Tablespoons sweetener—honey *or* sugar
6	Bags *or* 6 tablespoons loose raspberry herbal tea
2	Limes, quartered and squeezed
2	Quarts cranberry juice
1	Lime, sliced *or* wedged, to garnish

❶ In saucepan bring water and sweetener to a boil.

❷ In a gallon glass container, place raspberry tea. Squeeze 2 limes on top of tea leaves. Add lime quarters. Pour boiling water mixture over tea and limes. Cover container and steep tea for a minimum of 2 and a maximum of 24 hours. Strain tea or remove bags and limes.

❸ Add 2 quarts of cranberry juice to the tea mixture. Stir well and taste. Add additional sweetener if desired. Serve over ice with a twist of lime.

I discovered this combination while experimenting with herbal teas one day. Try some experimenting on your own!

MINT-LEMON ICED TEA

Makes 1 gallon   Serves 16
Preparation time: 5 minutes
Steeping time: 2-3 hours

R E C I P E   T I P S

A great summer-day beverage. Vary by using limeade instead of lemonade and garnishing with a twist of lime.

D O - A H E A D   T I P S

Prepare the steeping tea mixture 2 to 3 hours before serving time and strain.

◆

4	Cups boiling water
$\frac{1}{2}$	Cup sweetener, honey *or* sugar
1	Cup fresh mint leaves
6	Lemons, halved and squeezed
2	Oranges, halved and squeezed
	Peel of one orange, grated (optional)
1	Quart Minute Maid Lemonade, made from concentrate according to can directions
1 $\frac{1}{2}$ - 2	Quarts cold water
1	Lemon, sliced *or* wedged, to garnish

❶ Heat water and sweetener to boiling.

❷ In a gallon glass container, pour sweetened boiling water over mint leaves. Add the juice of lemons, oranges, and optional orange peel. Let steep for 2 to 3 hours.

❸ Strain tea mixture. Add 1 quart of lemonade and enough cold water to make 1 gallon of tea. Sweeten to desired taste. Serve over ice with a twist of lemon.

My friend Wendy Bergman prepared this delicious tea for us to enjoy during a long hot afternoon at a horse show. It certainly hit the spot on that scorching summer day.

For a spicy taste, add a cinnamon stick while steeping the tea.

KAFFREE APPLE TEA COOLER

Makes 1 ½ quarts   Serves 4
Preparation time: 5 minutes
Steeping time: 3 minutes

R E C I P E   T I P S
This thirst-quenching cooler features Natural Touch Caffeine-free Kaffree®
Tea, which is available in most health food stores. Add a cinnamon stick
while steeping the tea for a spicy taste. Try serving this beverage hot. Vary by
adding other juice concentrates, such as raspberry, cranberry, lemonade, etc.

D O - A H E A D   T I P S
Can be made the day ahead and chilled until serving time.

◆

6   Natural Touch Kaffree Tea bags
4   Cups water
1   12-ounce can frozen apple juice concentrate
12   Ounces sparkling mineral water

❶ Bring water to boiling. Steep tea bags in boiling water for 3
minutes. Combine tea with apple juice concentrate and
sparkling water. Serve over ice garnished with lemon.

MINTY GRAPE ICED TEA

Makes 6 1-cup servings
Preparation time: 5 minutes
Steeping time: 7 minutes

R E C I P E   T I P S
This Minty Grape Tea is an unusually delicious flavor combination. For an
interesting variation, try it with white grape juice.

D O - A H E A D   T I P S
The tea can be steeped the day ahead. Add the chilled grape juice and club
soda just before serving.

◆

1 ½   Cups water
3   Lemon herbal tea bags
2   Tablespoons fresh mint leaves, wrapped in
      cheesecloth *or* place in a tea ball or holder
1   24-ounce bottle unsweetened grape juice, chilled
1 ½   Cups club soda, chilled
6   Sprigs fresh mint for garnish

❶ Bring water to boiling. Combine boiling water, tea bags, and
mint leaves; cover and steep 7 minutes. Discard tea and
mint; cover and chill.

❷ Add grape juice and club soda to tea just before serving. Pour
over ice cubes in serving glasses, and garnish with fresh mint
sprigs. Serve immediately.

Made with white grape juice – this drink is elegant enough for the fanciest party.

CATAWBA COOLER

Makes 8 1-cup servings
Preparation time: 5 minutes

◆

1   25.4-ounce bottle sparkling pink Catawba grape juice, chilled

3   Cups cranberry-apple juice, chilled

1   10-ounce bottle club soda, chilled

3   Tablespoons lime juice

     Orange slices

     Lime slices

     Lemon slices

❶ Combine first 4 ingredients in a serving pitcher just before serving; stir until well blended. Float orange, lime, and lemon slices in pitcher. Pour over ice in serving glasses and garnish with orange, lime, or lemon slices. Serve immediately.

FROSTY PEACH PLEASURE

Makes 8 1-cup servings
Preparation time: 5 minutes

◆

24   Ounces sparkling mineral water, chilled

24   Ounces peach nectar, chilled

1   Cup unsweetened orange juice, chilled

$\frac{1}{2}$ Cup unsweetened grapefruit juice, chilled

$\frac{1}{4}$ Cup fresh lemon juice, chilled

     Orange-rind spirals for garnish

❶ Combine first 5 ingredients in a large pitcher; mix well. Pour over ice cubes in serving glasses; garnish with orange-rind spirals.

GOLDEN APRICOT PUNCH

Makes 3 quarts   Serves 12
Preparation time: 5 minutes

◆

2 $\frac{1}{2}$ Cups canned water-packed apricots, pureed

2   Cups orange juice

1   Cup lemon juice

2   Quarts pineapple juice

❶ In large juice container, combine all above ingredients. Chill until serving time. Pour over ice and serve, garnished with lemon, orange, or pineapple wedges.

My husband's mother, Alice Adams, shared this recipe with me. It came from a 1949 cookbook from her brother's alma mater, Emmanuel Missionary College.

PINEAPPLE-MELON SLUSH

Makes 9 1-cup servings
Preparation time: 5 minutes

◆

1   Small cantaloupe, halved, seeded, peeled, and cut into chunks

1   20-ounce can crushed pineapple in juice, undrained

3   Cups club soda, chilled

     Fresh mint to garnish

❶ In blender, combine cantaloupe and pineapple. Cover; blend 1 to 2 minutes or until smooth. For each serving, pour $\frac{1}{2}$ cup cantaloupe mixture into an ice-filled glass. Add $\frac{1}{3}$ cup carbonated beverage; stir gently. Garnish with fresh mint. Serve immediately.

FROSTED STRAWBERRY-BANANA SPRITZER

Makes 3 quarts   Serves 12
Preparation time: 10 minutes

R E C I P E   T I P S
Other fruit combinations can replace the frozen strawberries. Keep the bananas, though. They add the smooth texture.

D O - A H E A D   T I P S
The bananas and strawberries can be blended ahead and frozen. This is nice if you are making spritzers for a large group. Just thaw out the preblended fruits, add the remaining orange juice and club soda and serve.

◆

2	Bananas, cut in chunks
1 $^1/_2$	Quarts orange juice
2	Cups frozen strawberries, partially thawed
24	Ounces club soda
	Whole strawberry with stem *or* orange slices to garnish

❶ In blender bowl, combine bananas with 1 cup of orange juice or enough juice to blend bananas smooth. Pour banana mixture into a 4-quart container.

❷ In same blender bowl, combine strawberries with 1 to 2 cups of orange juice and blend until smooth. Pour strawberry mixture in with banana mixture.

❸ Add remaining orange juice and mix. Chill until serving time.

❹ Add club soda just before serving. Pour over ice and garnish with strawberry *or* orange slices.

This punch was served at my wedding. Are you surprised that it's my favorite?

STRAWBERRY SPARKLER

Makes 2 8-ounce servings
Preparation time: 5 minutes

M E N U   T I P S
Serve this Strawberry Sparkler as an appetizer or as an ending with any special meal. Garnish with whole stemmed strawberries or lemon wedges.

D O - A H E A D   T I P S
This sparkler tastes best served immediately.

◆

1	Cup fresh *or* frozen strawberries
$^1/_2$	Cup fresh papayas, mangoes, apricots, *or* peaches, chopped
1	Ounce lime juice
	Sweetener of choice, to taste
10	Ounces sparkling apple juice
	Whole strawberries *or* lime wedges to garnish

❶ In blender, combine fresh or partially thawed strawberries, papaya, lime juice, sweetener if desired, and sparkling apple juice. Blend until smooth. Pour over crushed ice and garnish with a whole strawberry.

CITRUS PIÑA COLADA

Makes 2 quarts or 8 servings
Preparation time: 5 minutes

D O - A H E A D   T I P S
Mix everything but club soda together several days ahead if desired, and store in refrigerator. Add club soda just before serving.

◆

4	Cups orange juice
2	Cups pineapple juice
$^1/_4$	Cup Coco Lopez (coconut cream)
or $^3/_4$	Teaspoon coconut extract
2	Cups club soda
	Fresh pineapple wedges *or* orange circles to garnish

❶ In 2 $^1/_2$-quart container, combine pineapple juice and Coco Lopez; mix well. Add orange juice and mix well. For individual servings place ice in glass and fill $^2/_3$ full of juice. Pour club soda in each glass until full. Garnish with fresh pineapple wedges or orange circles.

Enjoy the cool refreshing taste of this Frosted Orange Jubilee Milkshake—a fat-free variation of an old favorite.

FROSTED ORANGE JUBILEE MILKSHAKE

Makes 4 1-cup servings
Preparation time: 5 minutes

R E C I P E   T I P S
This Orange Jubilee makes a great breakfast beverage, appetizer, snack, or dessert—in other words, it's good just about anytime!

D O - A H E A D   T I P S
Best prepared just before serving.

◆

8   Ounces frozen orange juice concentrate

2   Cups nonfat milk *or* tofu milk

2   Tablespoons honey (optional)

1   Teaspoon vanilla

12 ice cubes

Orange-peel spirals, to garnish

❶ In blender, place all ingredients except orange peel and blend at high speed about 30 seconds or until ice cubes are crushed.

❷ Pour into serving glasses and garnish with orange-peel spirals.

Kids love milkshakes, and you'll love giving them this healthful version.

SEA BREEZE COOLER

Makes 1 14-ounce serving
Preparation time: 2 minutes

D O - A H E A D   T I P S
Prepare just before serving.

◆

Ice

10 Ounces cranberry juice

2 Ounces pink grapefruit juice

1 Lime wedge

❶ In individual 14-ounce serving glass, partially filled with ice cubes, pour cranberry juice till glass is $^2/_3$ full, add grapefruit juice to the rim and squeeze the lime wedge over the top. Gently stir to blend flavors. Serve immediately.

The crisp flavor of lime adds an extra surprise to this refreshing drink.

MARGARITA SLUSH

Makes 6 1-cup servings
Preparation time: 5 minutes

M E N U   T I P S
Serve this drink to your guests while you put the finishing touches on your Mexican Fiesta dinner. Or save it to serve as a dessert drink.

◆

1 6-ounce can frozen lemonade concentrate

1 6-ounce can frozen limeade concentrate

2 Tablespoons powdered sugar *or* honey

3 Cups crushed ice

2 Cups club soda, chilled

Coarse salt (optional)

Lemon *or* lime wedges to garnish

❶ In blender, combine lemonade concentrate, limeade concentrate, sweetener, and crushed ice. Cover; blend until slushy consistency. Add club soda; stir gently. If desired, rub rim of each glass with lime slice and dip in coarse salt. Fill each glass with slush mixture. Serve garnished with lime or lemon wedges.

GAZPACHO FIZZ

Makes 6 1-cup servings
Preparation time: 8 minutes

M E N U   T I P S
This recipe is great served as an appetizer.

D O - A H E A D   T I P S
Make this recipe the day ahead and chill well. Add club soda just before serving.

◆

1 15-ounce can tomato sauce, salt-free

1 $^1/_2$ Cups tomato juice

2 Stalks celery, chopped

2 Green onions, chopped

1 Medium cucumber, peeled and seeded

2 Tablespoons lime juice

$^1/_4$ Teaspoon hot sauce

1 10-ounce bottle club soda, chilled

Lime wedges for garnish

❶ Combine first 7 ingredients in blender; process until smooth. Cover blender and chill thoroughly. Stir in club soda just before serving. Pour into glasses. Serve garnished with a twist of lime.

SWISS ALMOND ROMA

Makes 2 1-cup servings
Preparation time: 5 minutes

R E C I P E   T I P S
Serve this drink iced or hot—either way it is surprisingly good.

◆

4 Teaspoons Natural Touch Kaffree Roma® (a caffeine-free coffee alternative)

$^1/_2$ Cup water

$^3/_4$ Cup nonfat milk *or* tofu milk

1 Tablespoon carob *or* cocoa powder

2 Tablespoons honey *or* sugar

$^1/_4$ Teaspoon almond extract

❶ Combine all ingredients in a blender and blend on medium speed for 30 seconds. Serve over ice or heat and serve hot.

CRANBERRY TEA

Makes 12 1-cup servings
Preparation time: 10 minutes
Simmering time: 2 hours

D O - A H E A D   T I P S
This recipe can be made the day before and reheated just before serving. Be sure to allow 2 hours for simmering time.

◆

1	Bag fresh cranberries
2	Oranges, quartered
2	Lemons, quartered
5	Cinnamon sticks
10	Whole cloves
3	Quarts water
	Honey *or* sugar to sweeten to taste

❶ In large saucepan, place whole cranberries. Squeeze orange and lemon quarters into the pan; then drop in quarters. Add cinnamon sticks and cloves. Add 3 quarts of water and bring to a boil. Simmer for 2 hours. (Cranberries will pop open.)

❷ Strain tea. Taste and add desired sweetener; return strained tea to saucepan and serve hot.

Pictured on page 108

Olsa Baker shared this recipe with me. An avid skier, Olsa enjoys this spicy hot drink after a day on the slopes.

ORANGE-APPLE HERB TEA

Makes 4 1-cup servings
Preparation time: 5 minutes
Steeping time: 10 minutes

R E C I P E   T I P S
This full-flavored herb tea can be served hot or cold. To serve cold, just remove tea from heat when you remove the tea bags. Add chilled apple juice and orange circles. Serve over ice.

D O - A H E A D   T I P S
You can make this tea ahead of time and chill until serving.

◆

3	Orange-spice flavor herb tea bags
2	Cups water
1	Tablespoon honey
2	Cups apple juice
4	Orange slices

❶ In saucepan, bring water to boil and add tea bags. Cover; let steep 3 to 5 minutes. Remove tea bags. Stir in honey. Add apple juice and squeezed orange slices; mix well. Simmer for an additional 3 to 5 minutes. Serve tea hot.

SPICED APPLE DRINK

Makes 4 1-cup servings
Preparation time: 5 minutes
Simmering time: 15 minutes to 2 hours

D O - A H E A D   T I P S
I love this drink even better the next day. The cinnamon and cloves can be left in overnight.

◆

1	Quart apple juice
2	Cinnamon sticks
5	Whole cloves

❶ In saucepan, simmer apple juice with cinnamon sticks and cloves for at least 15 to 20 minutes or as long as 2 hours. Serve hot, garnished with cinnamon stick.

Merrill and I serve this Hot Spiced Apple Drink every year at our traditional New Year's Eve open house.

Cooking Without Dairy Products and Eggs

Surprise! Cooking without dairy products and eggs doesn't have to mean giving up flavor.

This special section is designed for those who, for reasons of health or dietary preference, choose to avoid dairy products and eggs, and/or to follow a diet that is very low in cholesterol and fat. I encourage all cooks, however, to experiment with these variations. It's easy to convert your favorite recipes to healthier, lower-fat, cholesterol-free, dairy-free, and egg-free versions.

Included is a selection of recipes for nondairy alternatives to milk, cheese, yogurt, cream, and egg products. These variations are referred to in many of the recipes in this book. Milk substitutes include delicious alternatives such as **Almond Milk** and **Cashew-Rice Milk**. Unbelievably good cream substitutes include **Cashew-Rice Cream**, **Tofu Whipped Cream**, and **Fruit Cream**. And there are even sour cream and mayonnaise substitutes, made with tofu.

For cheese lovers, there's a delicious nondairy Parmesan cheese substitute made from a combination of seasonings and ingredients; and a pimento cheese substitute that can be baked for a sliceable cheese, or used unbaked in macaroni and cheese, lasagna, pizza, and other favorite recipes.

For those who would like to eliminate certain spices and condiments from their diets, there are recipes for vinegarless ketchup and seasoning substitutes for cinnamon, chili powder, and chicken seasoning.

You'll be amazed at the incredibly good taste of these culinary impostors.

In my seminars I prepare each recipe two ways, using a dairy option and a nondairy, eggless option. Sometimes I do not tell the participants which recipe is which. When they are asked to choose a favorite, about 80 percent say they prefer the nondairy, eggless option. Most are completely shocked when they learn that tofu is the base for most of the dairy substitutes. Most people have tasted tofu only as an ingredient in Chinese stir-fried dishes, or they have had a bad experience when they tried to cook with it. This is often because the tofu they tried was rancid. To others, it sounds like a fanatical health food—sure to taste "funny," and not worth the trouble. They couldn't be more wrong! Be sure to read all about tofu, beginning on page 12 in this book.

ALMOND MILK

Makes 6 cups
Preparation time: 10 minutes

R E C I P E   T I P S

This mouthwatering milk is wonderful over cereal, for drinking, or in recipes as a substitute for milk. Try replacing the almonds with cashews for a slightly different taste. Although the recipe suggests straining it, some like this almond milk just as well unstrained. If you plan to drink it "straight," I recommend straining it. You'll need a very good blender to get the almonds and sesame seeds perfectly smooth, which is essential if you do not strain the milk.

D O - A H E A D   T I P S

This milk can be made up to 5 days in advance and kept chilled in an airtight container.

◆

$3/4$	Cups almonds, blanched
1	Tablespoon honey
or 1	Dried pineapple ring, chopped
$1/4$	Cup sesame seeds
5	Cups water
$1/4$	Teaspoon salt
1	Teaspoon vanilla (use white vanilla for a whiter milk)

❶ In blender container, place almonds, dried pineapple if desired, sesame seeds, and a small amount of water. Blend until completely smooth. Add remaining water and the additional ingredients, and mix well.

❷ Line sieve with cheesecloth and pour the almond milk through the cheesecloth. Squeeze out remaining milk from cheesecloth. This will give the milk a totally smooth consistency. Chill before serving.

CASHEW-RICE MILK OR CREAM

Makes 4 $1/2$ cups milk or 2 $1/2$ cups cream
Preparation time: 5 minutes
Cooking time for rice: 35 minutes

R E C I P E   T I P S

Use leftover rice to prepare this recipe in just 5 minutes. The cream version can be used to thicken soups, gravies, and many other recipes. The milk can be used on cereal and in all recipes that call for milk.

D O - A H E A D   T I P S

This can be made up to 3 days ahead and stored in airtight container.

◆

$2/3$	Cup cooked rice, warm
$1/2$	Cup cashews, unsalted
1	Teaspoon vanilla (use white vanilla for a whiter cream)
$1/2$	Teaspoon salt
3 - 4	Teaspoons honey
3	Cups water for the milk *or* for cream use just enough water to blend the ingredients for a thicker consistency
1	Banana (use only if using cream for dessert-type recipes)

❶ In blender container, combine all ingredients and blend on high speed until smooth and creamy. It may take 2 to 3 minutes for the cashews to be thoroughly blended. Then add more water, a little at a time, until desired consistency is reached. For the cream, add as little water as possible to make a thick cream base for soups, gravies, and other recipes that need thickening. (Leave out the vanilla and the honey when using in soups.) For milk to use on cereals or in recipes, add the full 3 cups of water. Chill in airtight container.

TOFU WHIPPED CREAM

Makes 1 $1/2$ cups or 24 1-tablespoon servings
Preparation time: 5 minutes

RECIPE TIPS

This whipped cream alternative contains no cholesterol and only 40 calories per tablespoon. To get a result that resembles real whipped cream, it is important to use fresh, soft tofu. If you use firm tofu, you will need to add more water to blend. The result will resemble a softer whipped cream.

DO-AHEAD TIPS

This whipped cream can be made up to 3 days in advance and chilled. I like to make it a few hours before serving and chill it thoroughly if it is going to be eaten as a dessert topping. If you are using it as an ingredient in a recipe, you can use it immediately, without chilling.

◆

1	Cup soft tofu
4	Tablespoons vegetable oil
2	Tablespoons honey
$1/2$	Teaspoon lemon juice
$1/8$	Teaspoon salt
1 $1/2$	Teaspoons vanilla (use white vanilla for a whiter cream)

❶ Blend all ingredients in blender until smooth and creamy.

❷ Chill and serve as you would whipped cream.

This creamy topping will satisfy even the most discriminating taste buds.

TOFU SOUR CREAM

Makes 1 $1/4$ cups or 20 1-tablespoon servings
Preparation time: 5 minutes

RECIPE TIPS

This substitute can be used whenever your favorite recipes call for sour cream. A delicious, full-flavored alternative, it has only 44 calories per tablespoon. Check the expiration date to be sure you purchase fresh tofu.

DO-AHEAD TIPS

This sour cream can be made up to 5 days ahead and chilled in an airtight container.

◆

1	Cup soft tofu
4	Tablespoons vegetable oil
1	Tablespoon lemon juice
1 $1/2$	Teaspoons honey
$1/2$	Teaspoon salt

❶ Blend all ingredients until smooth and creamy. Use as a replacement for sour cream.

TOFU MAYONNAISE

Makes 1 $1/3$ cups or 20 1-tablespoon servings
Preparation time: 5 minutes

RECIPE TIPS

This delicious mayonnaise alternative can be used whenever mayonnaise is called for. Vary by adding herbs such as dill, basil, or rosemary for a delicious salad dressing or dip. Firm tofu will produce a thicker, more dip-like consistency.

DO-AHEAD TIPS

This recipe can be made up to 5 days in advance and chilled in an airtight container.

◆

1	Cup soft tofu, drained
4	Teaspoons lemon juice
4	Tablespoons light olive oil
1	Tablespoon sugar *or* honey
$3/4$	Teaspoon dry mustard
$1/2$	Teaspoon salt

❶ In blender or food processor, combine all ingredients and process for 1 minute or until smooth. Refrigerate until serving time.

FRUIT CREAM

Makes 1 $\frac{1}{2}$ cups or 6 $\frac{1}{4}$ cup servings.
Preparation time: 5 minutes
Cooking time: Allow time for cooking the cereal
or grain of choice.

R E C I P E   T I P S

Use leftover rice from dinner or oatmeal from breakfast. Just combine with the fruit juice and nuts or seeds to make a delicious fruit cream. Vary the grains, nuts, or seeds to create a variety of taste treats.

D O - A H E A D   T I P S

This cream can be made up to 5 days ahead and chilled in an airtight container.

◆

1   Cup fruit juice, such as unsweetened pineapple *or* apple juice

$\frac{1}{2}$ Cup cooked cereal *or* grain (oatmeal, rice, millet, etc.)

1   Tablespoon nuts *or* seeds (cashews, almonds, sunflower seeds, etc.)

❶ In blender container, combine $\frac{1}{2}$ cup of the juice with the cooked cereal or grain, and the nuts or seeds of choice. Blend until smooth and creamy. Add remaining juice, a little at a time, until mixture is of desired consistency. If additional sweetening is desired, add honey *or* blend 3 to 4 dates in with the cream until smooth. Chill and serve over hot cereal, waffles, pancakes, or as a dressing for fruit salad.

TARTAR SAUCE

Makes 2 $\frac{1}{2}$ cups
Preparation time: 5 minutes

R E C I P E   T I P S

Serve this recipe with Zucchini Crab Cakes from the dinner section, or whenever you would use tartar sauce.

D O - A H E A D   T I P S

This tartar sauce can be made ahead and refrigerated in an airtight container for up to 7 days.

◆

1   Cup soft tofu, mashed

$\frac{1}{4}$ Cup lemon juice

2   Tablespoons vegetable oil

2   Tablespoons sugar *or* honey

$\frac{3}{4}$ Teaspoon dry mustard

$\frac{3}{4}$ Teaspoon salt

$\frac{1}{2}$ Cup onion, chopped

$\frac{1}{4}$ Cup sweet pickle relish

❶ In blender container, combine all ingredients except pickle relish, and blend until smooth.

❷ Fold in pickle relish. Chill until serving time.

Use this delicious nondairy alternative whenever tartar sauce is called for.

SWEET AND SOUR SAUCE

Makes 2 $^3/_4$ cups
Preparation time: 5 minutes
Cooking time: 5 to 8 minutes

R E C I P E   T I P S
This recipe is delicious served over the Zucchini Crab Cakes
from the dinner section.

D O - A H E A D   T I P S
This sauce can be made up to 10 days ahead and refrigerated
in an airtight container.

◆

1 $^1/_2$	Cups unsweetened pineapple juice
$^1/_2$	Cup plus 2 tablespoons brown sugar
or $^1/_2$	Cup apple juice concentrate
$^1/_2$	Cup lemon juice
$^1/_2$	Teaspoon garlic powder
2	Tablespoons cornstarch
$^1/_4$	Cup soy sauce

❶ In small saucepan; combine all the above ingredients except
cornstarch. Add cornstarch to cold sauce mixture and whisk
until it is totally dissolved and no lumps remain.

❷ Cook over medium heat, stirring constantly, until mixture is
thickened.

VINEGARLESS TOMATO KETCHUP

Makes 2 cups or 32 1-tablespoon servings
Preparation time: 10 minutes
Cooking time: 30 minutes

R E C I P E   T I P S
Ordinary ketchup is high in vinegar, which can be an irritant to the
stomach. This version is made with lemon and orange juice instead. This
delicious ketchup beats out the brand-name kinds at our house.

D O - A H E A D   T I P S
It's easy to make a large amount of this recipe at once. It can be refrigerated,
frozen, or even canned, so you can always have a supply on hand.

◆

2	Cups canned tomatoes, crushed, *or* 2 cups fresh tomatoes, diced
1	4-ounce can tomato paste
$^1/_2$	Red sweet pepper, chopped
$^1/_4$	Cup onion, chopped
$^1/_8$	Cup frozen orange juice concentrate
1	Bay leaf
$^1/_2$	Teaspoon celery seed
2	Carrots, cut in chunks
4 - 6	Tablespoons lemon juice, to taste
	Salt to taste (optional)
	Garlic powder to taste

❶ In food processor, process all ingredients until smooth and
well blended.

❷ Transfer mixture to small saucepan and simmer uncovered
over medium-low heat, stirring constantly, to desired
consistency. Taste. Add more orange and/or lemon juice if
needed. If you prefer a sweeter flavor, add a small amount of
sugar or honey to taste.

NONDAIRY PIMENTO CHEESE

Makes 2 $^1/_2$ cups or 20 2-tablespoon servings
Preparation time: 10 minutes
Baking time for baked option: 1 hour

R E C I P E   T I P S

The noncooked version of this recipe is best used in dishes that will be cooked after the cheese has been added, such as pizza, macaroni and cheese, and lasagna. The cooked version is firmer and tastes delicious as a dip for vegetables and chips or as a spread for sandwiches. If you prefer the cooked version, but do not have time to soak the uncooked garbanzos, use 1 $^1/_2$ cups cooked garbanzos. This produces a thicker consistency, but not quite as thick as when you use presoaked, uncooked garbanzos.

D O - A H E A D   T I P S

This recipe will keep for up to a week in the refrigerator, or it may be frozen and thawed just before serving.

◆

$^1/_3$	Cup cashew nuts
$^2/_3$	Cup water
2	Ounces pimento, chopped
1	Teaspoon onion salt
1	Teaspoon garlic powder
1	Teaspoon paprika
$^1/_4$	Teaspoon savory
$^1/_8$	Teaspoon cumin
1	Teaspoon frozen orange juice concentrate
1	Teaspoon lemon juice
1 $^1/_2$	Cups precooked garbanzos, millet, *or* rice

❶ In blender container, combine cashews, pimento, seasonings, lemon and orange juice, and $^1/_2$ cup garbanzos, rice, or millet. Blend with just enough water to allow for blending. Mixture should be smooth and very thick.

❷ Add remaining garbanzos, rice, or millet, and just enough water to make of spreading consistency. Refrigerate in an airtight container.

Directions for Pimento Cheese to be precooked and used as a dip or spread or eaten by itself:

❶ Replace 1 $^1/_2$ cups cooked garbanzos, millet, or rice in the original recipe with 1 cup uncooked garbanzos that have been soaked for 24 hours. (For a quicker presoak, bring garbanzos to a boil for 5 minutes. Turn off burner and allow garbanzos to soak for 1 hour.)

❷ Combine all other ingredients in blender container. Add soaked uncooked garbanzo beans a few at a time with blender running until all the garbanzo beans are added.

❸ Place in loaf pan that has been generously sprayed with nonstick vegetable spray and bake at 400° F for 1 hour or until inserted knife comes out clean.

NONDAIRY PARMESAN CHEESE

Makes 1 cup or 16 1-tablespoon servings
Preparation time: 5 minutes

R E C I P E   T I P S

The flavor of Parmesan cheese is hard to imitate, but this recipe comes the closest to it of any I have tasted. It does not melt like the real thing, but when used in recipes where it is combined in a sauce or mixed in with other ingredients, it tastes very similar. It browns very quickly, so add it to the top of a dish only during the last few minutes of baking.

D O - A H E A D   T I P S

You can make larger amounts and refrigerate in an airtight container for approximately 2 weeks.

◆

$^1/_2$	Cup nutritional yeast flakes
$^1/_2$	Cup sesame seeds, ground
2	Teaspoons garlic powder
1	Teaspoon onion powder
2	Teaspoons McKay's Chicken-Style Seasoning
3	teaspoons lemon juice

❶ In blender container combine all ingredients except the lemon juice. Pour lemon juice on top of dry ingredients and blend until smooth. Refrigerate in an airtight container.

New Labels Make It Easier to Follow Dietary Guidelines

It makes good sense to read the labels on the foods you buy, and now new labels make it easier to shop smart and eat right. Already many food packages display nutrition labels that follow new regulations set by the Food and Drug Administration (FDA). These labels give more complete, accurate, and easy-to-understand information, including the following:

Serving sizes:

For the first time, serving sizes for similar foods must be consistent, making it easier to compare nutritional values.

Total calories and calories from fat:

The label must show both calories per serving and the number of calories from fat—information you need to budget fat intake.

Daily values for nutrients:

Given as percentages, daily values show the food's nutritional content based on a 2,000-calorie-a-day diet.

Calories per gram:

Tells how many calories are in each gram of fat, carbohydrate, and protein.

Recommended Dietary Guidelines

The Food and Drug Administration recommends that for an optimum diet to aid in the prevention and treatment of chronic diseases, we should comply with the following guidelines:

Total Fat:

No more than 30 percent of the total calories per day.

Saturated Fat:

No more than 10 percent of total calories per day.

Cholesterol:

No more than 300 milligrams per day (a little more than one whole egg).

Sodium:

No more than 2,400 milligrams per day.

Total Carbohydrates:

A minimum of 55 percent of total calories per day.

Simple Carbohydrates:

10 percent of total calories per day.

Complex Carbohydrates:

Minimum of 45 percent of total calories per day.

Fiber:

A minimum of 25 grams per day.

Protein:

12 to 15 percent of total calories per day.

A Peek Into My Pantry

Let's assume you've decided to make the transition to a healthful plant-based diet. What foods do you need to buy? Where do you buy them? Which brands are best? It isn't as overwhelming as it sounds. Let me show you what's in my pantry, refrigerator, freezer, and vegetable bin. If you gradually stock up on these items, you will have all the supplies you need for the fix-it-fast 30-minute meals in this book.

The first thing you'll see when you open my pantry door is my bread machine, and mill. There are several in the market but my choice is the Magic Meal DLX Kitchen Machine. You can write to Nutriflex, 1515 S. 400 West, Salt Lake City, Utah 84115, for information on how to purchase, **or** call 1-800-888-8587 or 1-801-467-0707. Mention this book and author when you call.

Grains

Rolled Oats – Both rolled oats and quick oats are used in this book.

Cornmeal – Whole grain is best, but most grocers sell only cornmeal that has the bran and germ removed. I like to use yellow cornmeal for the nice coloring it gives to food, but white cornmeal is equally nutritious.

Flour and Corn Tortillas – I purchase these in the refrigerator or freezer section of the supermarket. They keep well when frozen.

Popcorn – White hullless is my favorite.

Rice – I use long- and short-grain whole-grain brown rice and sweet rice. See page 10 for a detailed description of types of rice and how to prepare it.

Millet – Whole millet can be found in health food stores. It has much the same flavor as rice, but it is somehow refreshingly different.

Whole-Wheat Flour – I'm fortunate to have a kitchen mill for grinding my own flour. For breadmaking I use "hard" white winter wheat berries for milling. They have a higher gluten content, which produces the best-quality whole-wheat bread. If you are purchasing your flour already milled, choose a finely milled whole-wheat flour for the lightest bread. For pastry or other nonyeast baked products, choose an all-purpose or "soft" wheat flour. Its lower gluten content produces a more tender pastry. I keep all flours in the freezer to preserve their freshness and gluten content. (Be sure to bring the flour to room temperature before using it in baking.)

Wheat Gluten – Small amounts, added to yeast-activated baked goods, improves volume, texture, and shelf life.

Enriched Unbleached White Flour – I like to keep this on hand to combine with whole-wheat flour in some recipes.

Dough Enhancer – Add 1 tablespoon for every six cups of flour to give a light texture to yeast-activated baked goods. Contains soy flour and citric acid. Magic Mill is a good brand.

Wheat germ – Available raw or toasted, this product is the heart of the wheat, and adds a nice nutty flavor to many recipes. Toasted wheat germ has a longer shelf life and a nuttier flavor, but less nutrients than the raw. Be sure to store raw wheat germ in the freezer to maintain freshness.

Bulgur wheat – Available in health food stores and some supermarkets.

Pasta – I stock a variety of pasta shapes and sizes like linguini, vermicelli, angel hair, egg noodles, spirals, shells, etc. The nutritional analysis for the pasta recipes in this book is based on the standard white noodle. For a higher fiber diet, replace white noodles with whole-wheat pasta.

Nuts & Seeds

Get nuts and seeds at the grocery store or health food store or investigate your local co-op for a less expensive source. Buy them already roasted, or purchase them raw and roast them yourself in a shallow pan in a 300° F oven. Store large quantities of nuts and seeds in the freezer to preserve freshness.

Almonds – Raw, slivered and sliced,

Cashews – Unsalted, roasted

Peanut Butter – Be a label-reader. Buy peanut butter that lists only peanuts and salt on the label, and has no added oils, sweeteners, or preservatives.

Pecans – Raw, chopped

Sesame seeds – Hulled sesame seeds are white and have a milder flavor than the unhulled, brown kind. Both are fine for cooking

Tahini – This is a sesame seed paste or butter, made from ground, unhulled sesame seeds. It is a common ingredient in many traditional Middle Eastern dishes. You can buy it in some grocery stores and most health food stores. There is a recipe in this book to make your own tahini if you prefer. Tahini will separate, so be sure to mix in the oils before each use. Refrigerate after opening

Sunflower seeds – Buy these raw or dry roasted

Walnuts

Legumes

Most legumes are available dried or canned. Use either kind in the recipes in this book. Canned beans are more convenient, but they're more expensive, and may contain extra salt. They can be rinsed to lower the salt content. (See page 12 for detailed instructions on how to cook dried beans.)

Garbanzos (chickpeas)

Kidney Beans

Lentils

Pinto Beans

Red Beans

Tofu – This high-protein staple food is made from soybeans and can be used to replace dairy products and egg products. See page 12 for more detail on tofu—what types to buy, availability, and how to prepare.

Fruits

I purchase a variety of fresh fruits weekly – apples, oranges, seedless red grapes, bananas, and fruits in season. For a treat, we enjoy a mango or two each week. I love lemon or lime water and also like to use these fruits as a garnish, so I purchase 3 to 4 lemons and limes each week.

Dried Fruits – Watch out for fruits that are dried with sulfites. Many people are allergic to sulfites. I use a home food dehydrator, partially drying the fruits and then freezing them in airtight bags. This is a real treat.

Apricots (dried)

Coconut – I usually use the sweetened type and limit the quantity. However, the unsweetened type is better if you're trying to limit sugar. It is usually available only in health food stores.

Currants – These are a nice change from raisins.

Dates (seedless)

Raisins

Canned Fruits and Juices

Choose fruits that are juice-packed or have no added sugar. Choose fruit juices that have no added sugar and contain no additives.

Coco Lopez – This is the brand name for a pastelike coconut mixture that is often used for making mixed drinks, usually found with other drink mixers in the grocery store. You can substitute coconut extract for this, which is what I do most of the time.

Cranberry Juice

Lemon Juice

Peaches

Pears

Pineapple Chunks

Frozen Fruits and Juices

Be sure to buy juices that have no added sugar. When buying frozen fruits, get those that are loose-packed and quickly frozen without added sugar.

Apple Juice Concentrate – This concentrate is naturally very sweet, and can be used to flavor and sweeten many dessert recipes

Blueberries (whole)

Cranberry Juice Concentrate

Grape Juice Concentrate

Grapefruit Juice Concentrate

Lemon Juice Concentrate

Orange Juice Concentrate

Pineapple Juice Concentrate

Raspberries (whole)

Strawberries (whole or sliced)

Refrigerated Fresh Vegetables

Most fresh vegetables, of course, should be purchased as close to serving time as possible, so that you eat them at their peak of nutritive value and flavor. Depending on seasonal availability, I purchase 3 to 4 types of salad greens (usually green leaf lettuce, head lettuce, Bibb lettuce, and spinach), large beefsteak tomatoes, plum tomatoes, carrots, cabbage, cucumbers, avocados, mushrooms, scallions, fresh herbs, and other salad ingredients weekly. I use lots of broccoli, cauliflower, cabbage, zucchini, summer squash, and eggplant for a variety of vegetarian dishes. Fresh steamed vegetables can hardly be resisted by young and old alike.

Vegetable Bin Vegetables

There are a few fresh vegetables that keep well and can be bought ahead. These will last up to a month if refrigerated.

Garlic Cloves – For my family of five, I go through 3 to 4 bulbs per week. When you cut back on salt you will find that garlic is a great replacement

Onions (white, yellow, and sweet)

Potatoes – I like Russet potatoes for baking, and new red potatoes for boiling or steaming. I keep a supply of nice white cooking potatoes on hand for use in recipes in which potatoes will be combined with other foods.

Frozen Vegetables

I keep a supply of frozen vegetables in the freezer just in case I run out of a fresh vegetable.

Broccoli

Cauliflower

Carrots (sliced and baby whole)

Corn

Green Beans

Peas

Spinach (chopped)

Canned Vegetables

Because of the hidden salt usually found in them, I use very few canned vegetables. Tomato paste is the exception. I make my own canned roma tomatoes for delicious Italian sauce.

Artichoke Hearts – Canned artichoke hearts are available marinated or unmarinated. Unmarinated hearts are the lowest in salt and fat.

Basil – I have found a canned fresh water-packed basil that is a great alternative to fresh basil when the fresh is not available.

Capers – A small marinated bean that I use in small amounts in such recipes as Tuscany-Style Pasta Toss.

Ketchup (try the recipe for vinegarless ketchup in the variation section)

Green Chilies (chopped)

Olives (black)

Pimentos (chopped)

Roasted Red Peppers – If you are too busy to roast your own, these canned whole roasted red peppers are great to fall back on.

Tomatoes (canned whole with low salt)

Tomatoes (chopped canned)

Tomato paste (low salt)

Textured Vegetable Protein Products

Worthington Foods, Loma Linda® Foods, Morningstar Farms®, and Natural Touch® are all name brands of canned and frozen meat substitutes. These products, called "textured vegetable proteins," are made from gluten (protein from wheat flour) and soy products. They are free of animal fat, cholesterol, and preservatives. They are typically lower in fat—especially saturated fat—and calories than their meat and egg counterparts. These foods add a nice meatlike flavor and texture to recipes, and satisfy the preferences of those committed to vegetarian diets. They are available in natural food stores and grocery stores, nationally.

Dairy Products and Substitutes

Read labels carefully. Buy low-fat milk, cheeses, and sour creams. Skim milk and part skim cheeses have the very lowest fat content. Remember that even 2 percent milk is really 32 percent fat and that 1 percent milk is really 16 percent fat. Only skim milk is fat-free. The nutrition analysis in this book are based on using skim milk and part-skim cheeses in the recipes. For the nondairy substitutes, look in the variation section. You'll find recipes for cheese and Parmesan cheese, milks, creams, etc.

Eggs – Lacto-ovovegetarians and others who need to lower fat and cholesterol in their diets may actually use more eggs than normal. This is because they discard the yolks to eliminate cholesterol, and double up on the healthier whites,

Worthington Scramblers® and **Better 'n Eggs®** – Good cholesterol-free egg alternatives, made from egg whites

Evaporated Skim Milk – Although it comes in a can, don't confuse this with canned sweetened condensed milk—a totally different and much less healthy product. Canned evaporated skim milk is a good replacement for cream or half-and-half in recipes. You can even use it to make an acceptable substitute for whipped cream. Just refrigerate it until it is very cold, then add a little sweetener and vanilla and whip it at high speed with an electric mixer for about six minutes. You'll never miss the extra fat.

Mozzarella Cheese, Part Skim – This is a good low-fat cheese. It can be bought ahead, grated, and frozen for future use.

Parmesan Cheese – Although this cheese is high in fat, a tiny bit adds a lot of flavor and can be substituted for a much larger portion of other cheeses in recipes. In the variation section there is a substitute for Parmesan cheese.

Powdered Tofu milk – I like this as a replacement for dairy milk. It has a smoother texture and better flavor than soy milk. The brands I like are Tofu White, by Magic Mill, and Better Than Milk. These are available at health food stores. Use this milk when you wish to replace dairy milk in recipes, over cereal, and for drinking.

Seasonings and Herbs

I prefer to use fresh herbs whenever possible for their wonderful flavor. Dried herbs should be stored in the refrigerator or freezer and used within a few months of purchasing. Just before adding either dried or fresh herbs to a recipe, crush them in your hands to release their flavor. Try your hand at an herb garden, starting from small plants available at many garden shops.

Basil Leaves (fresh, dried, or canned)

Celery Seed (ground)

Celery Leaves (crushed)

Chives

Chili Powder

Cinnamon (ground and whole sticks)

Coconut Extract

Coriander

Cumin

Dillweed (chopped)

Garlic Powder

George Washington Broth Mix – This powdered broth mix comes in Beefy Brown, Golden, or Onion flavoring, and is available at health food stores and some grocery stores. It has a vegetable oil base with no animal fat added

Lemon Peel (grated)

McKay's Chicken-Style Seasoning – This is an excellent chicken-flavored seasoning for broth and soups. It has a vegetable oil base with no animal fat added. It is available at health food stores.

Mizo (soybean paste) – An Oriental flavoring, available at Oriental or health food stores.

Mustard (dried)

Nutritional Yeast Flakes – This is edible brewer's yeast *(Saccharomyces cerevisiae)* in flake form. Don't confuse it with the brown, powdered brewer's yeast product, which is very bitter. These yeast flakes are yellow and have a cheese-like flavor. I use them for seasoning popcorn and wherever a cheese flavor is wanted. I use the brand name Kal.

Old Bay Seasoning – A blend of herbs and spices developed for seafood, this seasoning mix is also good with many vegetarian dishes.

Onion Powder

Oregano Leaves (chopped) – There are two types of oregano, Italian and Mexican. They are very different in taste. Use Italian with Italian foods, and Mexican with Mexican foods.

Paprika – I prefer Hungarian paprika for its nice red color.

Parsley (chopped)

Poppy Seeds

Rosemary

Sage

Salt

Savory

Soy Sauce (low salt)

Thyme

Turmeric – Used to season and add yellow color to foods.

Vanilla Extract (white and regular) – White vanilla is nice when flavoring white or light-colored foods, such as ice cream or whipped toppings. It is available in grocery stores in the cake decorating section. The flavor is the same as regular vanilla. Be sure to use pure vanilla, not imitation.

Miscellaneous

Active Dry Yeast – Dry yeast comes in two types—regular and rapid rise. If you use instant yeast, you let the bread dough rise only once in bread tins. Be sure to read the label carefully to know which yeast you are buying. Use the yeast by the date listed on the package for the best results. Store in refrigerator or freezer to maintain freshness

Brown Sugar

Cornstarch – This is used for thickening sauces, soups, and gravies

Carob Chips – Carob is the ground dried fruit of the carob tree, which grows mostly in the Mediterranean region. Because products made from carob resemble chocolate, some people consider the fruit a chocolate substitute. Carob does not taste as rich as chocolate, but it has its own unique and pleasant flavor. It is low in fat, low in calories, and contains no caffeine. It is naturally sweet and contains fiber, calcium, phosphorus, and potassium. Carob is available in several forms: as powder, sweetened or unsweetened carob chips, in blocks for baking or cooking, and in powdered mixes for hot carob beverages. Carob chips are available at some grocery stores and all health food stores. I use the sweetened carob chips for most of my recipes.

Club Soda – A low-calorie carbonated beverage that makes a nice addition to punches.

Honey (raw) – Raw honey is fructose sugar. While some studies indicate honey as a preferable alternate to sugar, caloriewise and for the diabetic they are the same. Check the labels when buying honey. Raw honey may be available only in your health food store. Note: there have been warnings about giving infants (under 1 year old) raw honey, because of a few cases of food poisoning in infants. Be sure to consider this if serving to infants.

Molasses – Store molasses at room temperature before opening; then keep it in the refrigerator, where it will keep for up to three months. Molasses is available in both light and dark, or blackstrap versions. I prefer the milder flavor of light molasses.

Nonstick Vegetable Cooking Spray – I use a nonstick spray (such as Pam) for oiling baking pans or preparing a skillet for sautéing. It is a good way to save on fat without sacrificing flavor.

Tapioca – Instant brands are the most convenient.

Vegetable Oils

Keep all oils in the refrigerator—Oil kept on the pantry shelf can turn rancid and lose its fresh flavor.

Canola Oil – Canola oil is made from rape seed. Like olive oil, it is high in monounsaturated fat, which studies show is the preferred type of fat to lower cholesterol. It is a mild-tasting vegetable oil that does not break down at high temperatures and can be used in all types of cooking. It is fast gaining popularity in the supermarket

Olive Oil (cold-pressed) – This oil is high in monounsaturated fat—a good choice for fighting cholesterol. There are several varieties, from light all the way to extra-virgin, which is almost green with the color of the olives, and has the strongest taste. I prefer the taste of light olive oils for most cooking. The extra-virgin is perfect for a hearty tomato sauce.

Measurement Equivalents

3 teaspoons =1 Tablespoon (15 ml)

16 Tablespoons =1 Cup (about 250 ml)

4 Tablespoons =$\frac{1}{4}$ Cup (about 50 ml)

$\frac{1}{3}$ Cup=5 $\frac{1}{3}$ Tablespoons (about 80 ml)

2 Cups =1 Pint (about 500 ml)

4 Cups (2 pints) =1 Quart (about 1 L)

4 Quarts (liquid) =1 Gallon (about 4 L)

Substitutions

Many of the recipes you are currently using can be adapted to lower their fat content and improve their nutritional value. Experiment to find the alternatives you like best.

Whole Eggs

Replace 1 whole egg with 2 egg whites, or with Morningstar Farms Better'n Eggs® for recipes that do not need leavening, or with $\frac{1}{4}$ -$\frac{1}{3}$ cup blended tofu (both are cholesterol-free alternatives).

Sugar

Replace 1 $\frac{1}{4}$ cups sugar plus $\frac{1}{4}$ cup liquid with 1 cup honey.

Whole Milk

Replace 1 cup fresh whole milk with 1 cup nondairy milk alternative, such as tofu milk, Almond Milk, or Cashew-Rice Milk (recipes in variation section).

Sour Cream

Replace sour cream with Tofu Sour Cream (a cholesterol-free, low-fat alternative; recipe in variation section).

Whipped Cream

Replace whipped cream with Tofu Whipped Cream (a cholesterol-free, low-fat alternative; recipe in the variation section).

Mayonnaise

Replace mayonnaise with Basic Mayonnaise (a cholesterol-free, low-fat nondairy alternative; recipe in the variation section).

How the Recipes Are Analyzed

Calories per serving and a nutrient breakdown are included for every recipe. The dairy option and the nondairy for each recipe are calculated separately. The nutrients listed include grams of carbohydrate, protein, fat, and fiber. The fat is broken down in polyunsaturated, monounsaturated, saturated, and total fat. The nutrients listed in milligrams include cholesterol, sodium, potassium, iron, and calcium.

The recipes were developed for people who love good food, but who are also interested in lowering their intake of calories, sugar, fat, cholesterol, and sodium to maintain healthful eating patterns. The levels of these restricted nutrients in some recipes may be higher than those prescribed by a physician for specific health problems. The calorie and nutrient breakdown of each recipe is derived from computer analysis, based primarily on information from the U.S. Department of Agriculture. The values are as accurate as possible and reflect the following assumptions:

1. All nutrient breakdowns are listed per serving.

2. When a range is given for the number of servings (example: serves 6 - 8), the analysis is calculated on the larger number of servings.

3. When a range is given for an ingredient (example: 3 - 3 $\frac{1}{2}$ cups flour) the analysis is calculated on the lesser amount.

4. When ingredients are stated as "optional" or "to taste," they have been deleted from the nutrient information.

5. When a recipe gives the option of using oil or water, the analysis is based on using water.

6. When the recipe gives the option of baking in a pan coated with nonstick vegetable spray or lightly sautéing in oil or nonstick vegetable spray, the analysis will be based on the baking option.

7. When the recipe calls for honey or sugar, the analysis will be based on honey.

8. When the recipe calls for a choice of honey, sugar, or fruit juice, the analysis will be based on fruit juice.

Complete Nutritional Analysis by Recipe

RECIPE	SERVING	Calories	Pro gm	CHO gm	Fiber gm	Fat-Total gm	Fat-Saturated gm	Fat-Mono gm	Fat-Poly gm	Chol mg	Vit A-Caro RE	Vit C mg	Ca mg	Iron mg	Phosp mg	Potassium mg	Sodium mg
Breakfast																	
Granola Parfait	1	236	7.82	35	3.99	8.83	1.65	2.41	4.44	1.02	175	28.7	143	1.51	228	558	52.1
Granola Parfait, Nondairy	1	338	7.92	37.2	4.49	19.8	3.02	5.02	10.8	0	179	28.5	74.2	3.71	180	468	56.4
Granola	½ cup	274	7.54	32.8	5.26	13.6	3.87	4.03	4.85	0	19.5	18.6	26.6	2.24	246	348	101
Muesli	½ cup	190	7.02	29.8	5.28	5.77	0.691	3.16	1.46	0.138	54.5	1.56	49.2	2.17	214	320	7.24
Hot Spiced Oatmeal	½ cup	253	11	44.5	5.12	4.47	0.749	2.13	1.15	2.93	4.95	3.64	237	1.59	321	510	358
Smoothie	1 cup	211	8.08	43.2	2.98	1.88	0.982	0.427	0.228	5.86	8.34	48.8	261	0.563	223	671	98.8
Smoothie Nondairy	1 cup	211	14.8	25.1	4.55	7.73	1.18	1.6	4.04	1.1	19.8	48.5	222	7.48	237	686	48.7
Cornmeal Hearts and Stars	2 pieces (½ cup)	85.3	1.8	18.8	5.46	0.886	0.088	0.177	0.442	0	15.2	15.4	17.3	0.89	44.1	137	276
Fruit Toast	1 piece	216	4.8	49.3	5.16	1.65	0.444	0.518	0.435	0	70.7	7.23	39.6	1.86	124	409	223
Oat Pancakes	2 pancakes	270	8.98	52.2	5.65	3.57	0.498	1.55	1.08	0	2.36	0.124	33.2	2.87	218	210	540
Fruited Cream	½ cup	111	5.71	22.4	0.85	0.24	0.093	0.061	0.053	2.29	20	47.5	189	0.36	132	293	75.1
Fruited Cream, Nondairy	½ cup	194	4.24	21.7	1.35	11.2	1.46	2.66	6.45	0	23.7	47.1	48	2.43	47.9	136	49.5
Garden Vegetable Tortilla, Dairy	1 tortilla	228	17	26.2	2.87	7.88	0.451	1.21	1.13	0.357	37.3	17.4	51.3	2.45	115	438	417
Garden Vegetable Tortilla, Nondairy	1 tortilla	241	14.9	26.7	3.62	10.8	0.88	1.86	2.81	0.357	42.9	17.5	112	5.75	167	418	312
Italian Frittata	3" wedge	241	29	29.9	3.58	0.579	0.11	0.052	0.249	0.138	212	81.7	68.3	2.2	105	846	417
Italian Frittata, Nondairy	3" wedge	260	19.7	29.1	5.82	9.46	1.39	2.01	5.27	0	229	81.8	254	12.2	277	779	310
Lunch																	
Peanut Butter Surprise	1 sandwich	389	13.7	47	5.04	18.8	3.69	8.46	5.29	0	5.85	8.65	89.7	2.69	217	457	457
Lunch Box Burritos	1 burrito	279	16.5	32	5.26	10.3	1.23	2.07	1.13	4.09	12.8	2.89	128	2.74	94.6	381	624
Gopher Sandwich	1 pita half	167	5.62	24.6	1.29	5.77	0.954	2.19	2.23	0	0	0.108	29.4	0.995	87.1	119	208
Avocado Sunshine	1 sandwich	385	9.4	52	14.7	18.2	3.02	10.6	2.75	0	112	29.3	115	3.92	198	1071	327
Avocado Sunshine, Nondairy	1 sandwich	386	11.4	44.3	15	21.2	3.44	12.2	3.58	0	115	30.3	141	5.27	223	1104	431
Waldorf Chicken Salad	1 pita half	261	9.36	40.3	3.64	7.61	0.335	1.65	0.772	0	2.99	5.02	43.8	1.03	60.9	170	392
Waldorf Chicken Salad, Nondairy	1 pita half	293	11.4	32.3	3.94	14.2	1.2	3.24	4.61	0	5.23	5.2	70	2.38	85.1	203	416
Brown Rice Citrus Sandwich	1 pita half	211	5.7	43.9	2.35	1.45	0.317	0.505	0.501	0.511	15.6	7.09	78.7	0.955	209	268	33.8
Brown Rice Citrus Sandwich, Nondairy	1 pita half	262	5.75	45	2.6	6.92	1	1.81	3.7	0	17.5	7	44.1	2.06	184	223	36
Protose Pita Sandwich	1 pita half	209	15.8	25.1	1.2	5.33	0.182	0.405	0.576	0.17	13.6	4.46	74.5	3.56	66	208	412
Protose Pita Sandwich, Nondairy	1 pita half	226	15.8	25.4	1.29	7.15	0.411	0.84	1.64	0	14.2	4.43	63	3.93	58	193	413
Garbanzo Delight Sandwich	1 sandwich	224	10.3	43	8.42	2.49	0.291	0.548	1.12	0.32	550	12.9	77.7	3.44	223	559	200
Pecan Meatball Hoagie	1 hoagie	500	21.5	68.7	11	18.9	2.6	10.2	4.43	2.83	447	61	168	5.77	393	1996	631
Pecan Meatball Hoagie, Nondairy	1 hoagie	508	18.3	68.7	11.9	22.2	2.88	10.9	6.46	1.17	454	61.1	222	9.76	410	1991	410
Grilled Eggplant-Tomato Sandwich	1 sandwich	147	8.09	26.9	5.38	1.95	0.537	0.57	0.522	1.02	58.9	18.9	156	1.81	213	501	350
Grilled Eggplant-Tomato Sandwich, Nondairy	1 sandwich	256	8.84	25.5	5.99	15.1	2.2	3.71	8.2	0	63.5	19.9	95.9	4.43	173	422	410
Falafel With Tahini Sauce	1 pita half	187	8.17	24.4	5.18	7.16	1	2.41	3.1	0.477	19.5	5.76	98.3	3.12	199	276	68
Falafel With Tahini, Nondairy	1 pita half	198	8.25	24.3	5.24	8.48	1.17	2.73	3.87	0.375	19.9	5.86	92.3	3.38	195	268	85.3
Oven-cured Tomatoes	½ plum tomato	9.7	0.371	2.17	0.538	0.137	0.019	0.021	0.056	0	25.5	7.83	2.53	0.207	10.3	92.4	92.6
Circular Sub	1 3" wedge	192	6.32	24.6	3.73	7.96	1.2	1.85	2.86	0.991	116	29.3	45.4	1.77	66	244	356
Minestrone Soup	2 cups	158	6.74	26.1	6.8	4.24	0.589	2.6	0.645	0	691	35.4	86.8	3.21	143	885	94.7
Vegetable Soup	2 cups	212	8.89	33.8	8.19	6.08	1.15	2.66	1.87	0	328	29.4	50.2	2.17	179	792	56.8
Millet Mushroom Soup	1 ¼ cups	61	2.28	13.2	2.07	0.469	0.075	0.073	0.216	0	87.4	28.5	32.5	1.05	61.5	359	367
Corn Chowder	1 ¼ cups	216	7.72	48.2	4.98	0.319	0.104	0.046	0.107	1.53	21.4	25	140	0.843	176	754	59.8
Corn Chowder, Nondairy	1 ¼ cups	290	6.87	56.4	5.73	5.59	1.11	3.16	1.01	0	21.4	24.5	25.8	1.68	160	688	192
Cream of Broccoli Soup	1 ¼ cups	88	5.42	11.1	2.72	3.26	0.583	1.06	1.39	1.15	131	80.8	142	1.01	128	426	115
Cream of Broccoli Soup, Nondairy	1 ¼ cups	168	7.2	20.9	3.29	7.28	1.38	3.41	2.07	1.15	131	80.8	149	1.72	178	483	251
Tomato Corn Chowder	1 cup	150	11	19.9	2.29	3.56	0.491	0.836	2.03	0.816	61.5	16.6	90.9	1.28	82.3	431	245
Tomato Corn Chowder, Nondairy	1 cup	140	9.86	17.7	2.38	3.95	0.512	0.896	2.21	0	62.2	16.3	26.1	1.35	49.3	388	222
Spinach Tofu Soup	1 cup	91	4.15	15.3	2	1.75	0.28	0.43	0.88	0	340	8.4	62	2.32	94.05	240	601

Complete Nutritional Analysis by Recipe

RECIPE	SERVING	Calories	Pro gm	CHO gm	Fiber gm	Fat-Total gm	Fat-Saturated gm	Fat-Mono gm	Fat-Poly gm	Chol mg	Vit A-Caro RE	Vit C mg	Ca mg	Iron mg	Phosp mg	Potassium mg	Sodium mg
Chilled Cucumber Soup	1 ½cups	92.4	8.92	14.3	2.29	0.585	0.233	0.121	0.118	2.83	320	21.8	316	1.88	237	701	139
Chilled Cucumber Soup, Nondairy	1 ½cups	237	9.34	9.84	3.39	19.5	2.52	4.52	11	0	329	22.3	138	5.81	140	573	338
Borscht	1 ½cups	76.9	2.39	17.4	3.27	0.382	0.06	0.045	0.157	0	465	33.9	58	1.16	56.9	539	298
Beef Vegetable Stew	1 cup	99	9.5	13.9	1.74	0.71	0.03	0.01	0.059	0	513.5	6.45	17.25	2.15	37.55	224	295
Herb Tomato Soup	1 ½cups	66.8	1.58	9.28	2.2	3.25	0.546	1.08	1.37	0.042	581	20.4	50.3	1.06	39.8	368	104
Chicken Noodle Soup	1 ½cups	208	7.88	28.2	4.26	7.18	0.412	1.88	1.11	21.1	611	6.19	23.1	1.33	72.7	252	442
Herbed Pasta Salad	1 cup	154	2.68	14.2	4.21	10.6	1.04	6.36	2.53	0	276	32.6	38.3	1.56	47.2	261	276
Citrus Rice Salad	1 cup	216	5.79	40.2	3.02	4.55	0.513	2.56	1.19	0.818	27.3	15	117	0.95	171	348	47.8
Taco Salad	1 cup	140	4.53	17.5	4.43	6.81	1	3.94	1.34	0.033	279	59.1	56.9	2.07	80.9	434	318
Spinach Salad Supreme	1 cup	184	3.84	25.2	4.45	9.33	0.778	5.53	2.5	0	482	32	94.7	2.59	89.9	544	59.1
Raspberry-Asparagus Spinach Salad	1 ½cups	285	18.6	29.3	11.8	10.4	2.41	3.44	4.9	0	607	65	105	3.04	95.6	873	260
Chefs Salad	1 ½cups	232	8.15	29.5	12.4	10.7	1.6	5.6	1.94	0.19	607	32.8	75.5	3.54	170	900	132.5
Herbed Garden Salad	2 cups	142	5.94	22.3	8.01	5.22	0.559	2.82	1.33	0	2294	51.1	162	3.37	157	1022	49.2
Fruit Slaw	4 cups	119	0.974	22.9	2.73	3.68	0.474	0.844	2.09	0	399	34.3	32	0.549	22	263	12.2
Tabouli Salad	1 ½cups	123	3.1	18.5	5.29	4.97	0.689	3.37	0.572	0	31.3	16.7	22.1	0.876	78	280	187
Mango and Chickpea	½cup	220.5	9.1	39.8	10.5	4.12	0.457	1.88	1.26	0.338	102.5	9.7	89	2.4	206	458.5	59
Mango and Chickpea, Nondairy	½cup	257	9.35	39.35	10.7	8.5	1	2.91	3.8	0	104	10	69	3.26	192.5	432.5	116.5
Italian Herb Dressing	1 tbsp	40.5	0.023	0.332	0.014	4.46	0.603	3.28	0.376	0	0.287	0.951	1.02	0.032	0.549	3.82	0.214
Lemon Garlic Dressing	1 tbsp	62.1	0.053	0.783	0.033	6.75	0.916	4.97	0.573	0	0.152	3.62	1.22	0.034	1.11	10.9	0.143
Light Vinaigrette	1 tbsp	7.22	0.023	2.03	0.015	0	0.002	0	0.004	0	0.087	2.02	0.664	0.012	0.382	6.43	76.5
Poppy Seed Dressing	1 tbsp	80.2	0.153	4.9	0.083	7	0.941	5	0.739	0	0.048	1.31	8.92	0.11	6.05	13.4	33.8
Tahini Dressing	1 tbsp	33.7	1.19	1.45	0.475	2.83	0.403	1.07	1.24	0.085	0.378	0.702	17.1	0.327	47.2	37.6	3.78
Hummus Dip	4 tbsp	242	11.7	34.4	10.8	7.47	0.931	2.32	3.3	0	4.48	5.86	68.9	3.86	255	513	13.1
Spicy Citrus Dressing	1 tbsp	38.1	0.061	5.81	0.059	1.95	0.143	1.14	0.587	0	2.68	4.11	1.98	0.074	1.08	15.2	0.426
Apricot Yogurt Dressing	1 tbsp	29.7	0.718	2.31	0.134	2.07	0.274	0.504	1.19	0.204	11.8	0.852	23.4	0.089	19.8	53.7	8.85
Apricot Yogurt Dressing, Nondairy	1 tbsp	51.7	0.868	2.02	0.256	4.71	0.606	1.13	2.73	0	12.7	1.05	11.4	0.613	11.8	37.8	43.6
Nondairy Ranch Dressing	1 tbsp	21.9	1.02	0.378	0.157	1.94	0.269	1.12	0.449	0	1.14	0.526	13.6	0.679	12.4	17.3	54.2
Creamy Basil Dressing	1 tbsp	29.7	0.655	1.22	0.041	2.56	0.356	1.87	0.216	0.192	1.54	1.56	25	0.089	17.9	36.8	8.22
Creamy Cucumber Dressing	1 tbsp	17	0.78	0.58	0.22	1.4	0.195	0.803	0.325	0	1.36	1.01	11.25	0.52	10.57	28.67	38.96
Guacamole	¼cup	175	2.43	11	10.15	15.5	2.46	9.65	1.99	0	68.5	14.75	17.25	1.13	53	675	278.5
Dinner																	
Chicken à la King	2 cups	440	13.9	72.3	7.2	11	1.61	4.73	3.93	2.65	382	17.2	88.1	3.96	347	444	348
Chinese Cashew Caserole	1 cup	239	6.12	24	2.78	14.2	2.51	6.93	3.21	10.9	3.27	2.25	25.6	2.26	152	224	257
FriChik Wontons	1 wonton	89.7	4.4	11.8	2.04	2.74	0.127	0.174	0.17	13.2	96.7	0.696	6.91	0.701	31.5	45	107
Oriental Pepper Steak	2 cups	298	11.3	53.9	5.94	5.03	0.82	1.33	2.41	0	81.7	30.9	91.1	4.62	260	458	360
Oriental Tofu Peanut Sauce Over Rice	2 cups	367	17.1	52.2	5.94	11.2	1.91	3.73	4.87	0	15.1	3.97	157	7.46	319	364	573
Fillet of Fish Over Rice	2 cups	345	15.5	53.1	4.44	8.26	0.877	1.44	2.68	2.21	6.83	0.926	115	5.94	239	231	381
Zucchini Crab Cakes	2 crab cakes	83.6	3.77	15.3	1.12	0.827	0.188	0.271	0.193	0.833	14.7	3.9	27.9	0.87	38.8	149	498
Vegetarian Fajitas	1 fajita	252	11.5	29.3	2.93	11.2	1.08	2.72	3.3	0.24	107	22.9	70.5	2.99	85.4	289	347
Vegetarian Fajitas, Nondairy	1 fajita	262	11.5	28.4	3.01	12.8	1.29	3.12	4.26	0.24	108	23.1	77.1	3.32	91.4	297	364
Tostada Club	1 tostada	395	16.5	63.5	17.5	11.7	1.53	4.73	1.99	0	1613	187	218.5	12.4	306	1331	467
Vegetable Enchiladas	2 enchiladas	187	8.4	36.3	5.23	1.78	0.181	0.48	0.999	0	359	31.9	87.7	1.94	118	378	313
Vegetable Enchiladas, Nondairy	2 enchiladas	269	8.4	29.2	5.83	15.1	1.91	3.64	8.68	0	364	33.3	140	4.61	167	443	450
Spanish Sauce	½cup	22.1	0.623	5.19	0.765	0.156	0.027	0.026	0.067	0	33.9	10.2	17.4	0.365	14.3	137	79.7
Black Beans With Rice	2 cups	346	16.3	68.2	14.3	1.43	0.304	0.179	0.525	0	73.3	34.8	82.8	5.55	267	786	384
Black Beans With Rice, Nondairy	2 cups	351	16.3	67.7	14.3	2.26	0.412	0.377	1.01	0	73.6	34.9	86.1	5.72	270	790	392
Mazidra	2 cups	400	16.5	57.6	8.22	12.4	1.75	8.42	1.52	0	1.81	6.43	53.4	4.78	321	543	30.3
Tuscany-style Pasta	2 cups	209	6.74	40	3.78	2.77	0.376	1.36	0.566	0	865	30.8	49.5	2.62	106	325	129

RECIPE	SERVING	Calories	Pro gm	CHO gm	Fiber gm	Fat-Total gm	Fat-Saturated gm	Fat-Mono gm	Fat-Poly gm	Chol mg	Vit A-Caro RE	Vit C mg	Ca mg	Iron mg	Phosp mg	Potassium mg	Sodium mg
Pasta g Viola	2 cups	521	22.1	91.8	14.5	7.59	1.15	4.2	1.37	0	0	2.89	131	6.76	354	768	186
Linguine Vegetable Toss	2 cups	278	8.57	48.5	6.12	6.7	0.923	3.91	1.08	0	947	54.6	96	4.14	160	721	27.6
Zucchini Ziti	2 cups	311	12.4	52.4	4.68	6.48	0.874	2.22	2.68	4.72	111	34	58.6	3.97	126	624	524
Potato Primavera	1 potato	456	14.1	82.3	13.8	10.4	1.06	6.23	2.35	0	1372	114	150	5.24	332	1637	138
Grilled Potatoes and Vegetables With Roasted Garlic and Basil	2 cups	457	12	71.6	8.42	15.1	1.98	10.1	1.96	0.75	287	84.9	83.1	4.8	174	1097	480
New Red Potatoes and Vegetables	2 cups	273	17.9	38.9	3.39	4.95	2.95	1.31	0.322	16.4	559	51.2	220	1.88	199	526	539
New Red Potatoes and Vegetables, Nondairy	2 cups	364	11	23.9	4.6	27	3.54	6.36	15.5	0	568	54.1	142	7.16	165	633	681
Mediterranean Vegetable Blend	2 cups	214	20.1	24.3	4.43	5.19	0.582	2.53	0.557	0	248	50.7	92.3	3.84	78.9	640	556
Garlic-Herb Vegetable Bake	2 cups	219	5.13	36.2	5.04	7.38	1.02	5.03	0.827	0	104	44.5	55.6	2.64	134	986	21.5
Herb French Bread Pizza	2 2" pieces	251.6	8.1	44	4.87	4.8	0.87	1.72	1.26	1.28	932	31.4	90.5	4.16	111	722	957
Basic Whole-Wheat Bread	1 slice	106	4.25	22	3.9	2.8	0.38	0.62	1.56	0	0.06	0.02	10.9	1.23	108	130	91
Auto-bake Bread	1 slice	82.5	3.1	15.9	2.7	1.3	0.23	0.39	0.56	0	0.83	4	8.8	8.83	78.6	113	192

Drinks

RECIPE	SERVING	Calories	Pro gm	CHO gm	Fiber gm	Fat-Total gm	Fat-Saturated gm	Fat-Mono gm	Fat-Poly gm	Chol mg	Vit A-Caro RE	Vit C mg	Ca mg	Iron mg	Phosp mg	Potassium mg	Sodium mg
Raspberry Lime Iced Tea	8 oz	99.6	0.056	25.6	0.495	0.161	0.051	0.021	0.047	0	0.7	56.6	7.61	0.258	3.95	40.2	6.27
Mint Lemon Iced Tea	8 oz	67.5	0.284	18.2	0.209	0.031	0.016	0.009	0.033	0	4.69	20.6	8.99	0.199	5.77	73.2	7.8
Kaffree Apple Tea Cooler	12 oz	79.7	0.238	19.6	0.157	0.17	0.031	0.004	0.053	0	0	1.02	11.4	0.448	11.9	214	13.7
Minty Grape Iced Tea	8 oz	69	0.636	16.9	0.565	0.091	0.028	0.004	0.025	0	1.13	0.113	14.4	0.284	12.5	150	17.6
Catawba Cooler	8 oz	120	0.625	30.2	0.708	0.153	0.035	0.012	0.051	0	1.24	32.2	17	0.278	13.1	151	12.1
Frosty Peach Pleasure	8 oz	67.6	0.554	17.2	0.721	0.095	0.014	0.021	0.032	0	28.6	29.4	21.5	0.257	13.1	130	7.33
Golden Apricot Punch	8 oz	139	1.33	36.2	2.56	0.224	0.028	0.041	0.081	0	102	46.9	33.4	0.667	27.7	378	4.2
Frosted Strawberry Banana	8 oz	109	1.22	27.3	2.02	0.373	0.066	0.056	0.089	0	25.2	76.1	21.1	0.541	28.6	345	14.6
Pineapple Melon Cooler	8 oz	91.2	0.787	23.4	1.1	0.217	0.03	0.037	0.072	0	194	30.9	17	0.358	13.9	261	15
Strawberry Sparkler	8 oz	122	1.06	30.6	3.46	0.552	0.076	0.076	0.213	0	23.8	94.4	39.9	0.888	28.9	503	7.42
Citrus Piña Colada	8 oz	113	1.39	21.4	0.721	2.87	2.34	0.157	0.084	0	25.4	69.7	24.3	0.612	35.2	359	14.6
Sea Breeze Cooler	14 oz	183	0.285	46	1.08	0.34	0.101	0.045	0.096	0	1.69	122	13.6	0.539	14.2	143	6.24
Margarita Slush	8 oz	126	0.163	33	0.227	0.085	0.01	0.005	0.024	0	2.84	8.5	10.1	0.288	4.68	40.7	21.6
Gazpacho Fizz	8 oz	36.5	1.6	8.89	2.15	0.199	0.04	0.023	0.083	0	82.1	30.9	36.7	1.1	43	468	265
Frosted Orange Jubilee	8 oz	136	5.53	27.7	0.54	0.339	0.157	0.079	0.032	2.2	15.9	79.2	172	0.26	156	584	68.3
Frosted Orange Jubilee, Nondairy	8 oz	132	4.65	23.9	0.97	2.41	0.271	0.413	1.02	0	19.5	78	25.3	0.906	90.7	551	19.7
Hot Cranberry Tea	8 oz	25.7	0.294	6.61	1.31	0.098	0.016	0.024	0.049	0	5.75	18.8	9.51	0.124	6.68	74.1	7.4
Orange Apple Herb Tea	8 oz	74.1	0.09	18.8	0.15	0.136	0.023	0.006	0.041	0	0.1	1.17	11.3	0.498	9.02	150	7.54
Swiss Almond Roma	8 oz	104	3.34	24.7	1.06	0.186	0.111	0.05	0.013	1.65	0.032	1.12	127	0.244	96.4	189	51.2
Swiss Almond Roma, Nondairy	8 oz	101	2.69	21.9	1.38	1.74	0.196	0.3	0.757	0	2.73	0.218	17	0.728	47.7	164	14.8
Hot Spiced Apple Drink	8 oz	106	0.136	26.5	0.274	0.25	0.043	0.011	0.075	0	0.183	2.04	15.9	0.84	15.9	270	6.8
Spiced Herbal Orange Tea	8 oz	3.62	0.022	0.85	0.075	0.023	0.006	0.003	0.013	0	0.63	2.04	7.16	0.201	0.315	24.5	2.42

Desserts

RECIPE	SERVING	Calories	Pro gm	CHO gm	Fiber gm	Fat-Total gm	Fat-Saturated gm	Fat-Mono gm	Fat-Poly gm	Chol mg	Vit A-Caro RE	Vit C mg	Ca mg	Iron mg	Phosp mg	Potassium mg	Sodium mg
Fruit Medley With Apricot	1 cup	212	3.96	52.5	4.8	0.45	0.07	0.13	0.12	0.51	353	7.6	87	2.45	113	982	34.6
Fruit Medley With Apricot, Nondairy	1 cup	262	4.01	53	5	5.9	0.76	1.43	3.3	0	355	7.5	52.5	3.55	89	938	36.8
Peaches With Creamy Raspberries	1 cup	87.1	4.37	16	2.56	1.29	0.174	0.729	0.304	1.02	47.9	9.95	125	0.304	111	349	43.4
Peaches With Creamy Raspberries, Nondairy	1 cup	189	4.48	18.2	3.06	12.2	1.55	3.34	6.7	0	51.6	9.77	56.4	2.5	62.6	259	47.8
Peaches Supreme	1 cup	92.2	5.2	18	1.23	0.287	0.137	0.086	0.06	1.84	35.3	6.22	175	0.152	147	354	115
Peaches Supreme, Nondairy	1 cup	138	7.23	20.5	2.36	4.06	0.581	0.908	2.29	0	39.8	6.81	92.8	4.61	89.5	244	96
Pears in Orange Sauce	½ pear	123	0.693	31.7	2.37	0.415	0.031	0.085	0.101	0	10	27.6	16.6	0.385	17.7	203	136
Tropical Fruit Plate	1 cup	221	3.7	50.5	4.71	1.78	0.789	0.369	0.248	3.5	51	113	106	0.7	77.1	849	28.6
Tropical Fruit Plate, Nondairy	1 cup	213	7	43.2	5.46	3.87	0.658	0.781	1.9	0	55.7	112	111	4	88.1	850	10.4
Strawberry Parfait	1 cup	161	5.68	29	4.6	3.92	0.45	2.14	0.958	1.02	12	63.8	147	0.873	148	531	47.6
Strawberry Parfait, Nondairy	1 cup	262	5.78	31.3	5.1	14.9	1.82	4.75	7.36	0	15.8	63.6	78	3.07	99.8	441	52

RECIPE	SERVING	Calories	Pro gm	CHO gm	Fiber gm	Fat-Total gm	Fat-Saturated gm	Fat-Mono gm	Fat-Poly gm	Chol mg	Vit A-Caro RE	Vit C mg	Ca mg	Iron mg	Phosp mg	Potassium mg	Sodium mg
Apricot Whip	½ cup	257	6.77	44.5	3	7.55	1.03	1.74	4.24	0	141	1.48	93.6	5.18	104	574	55.8
Banana Mango Smoothie	1 cup	175	7.25	37.8	2.78	0.649	0.231	0.138	0.114	2.04	204	24.4	236	0.455	192	533	88.8
Banana Mango Smoothie, Nondairy	1 cup	379	7.46	42.3	3.78	22.5	2.98	5.35	12.9	0	212	24	97.5	4.86	95.6	353	97.5
Strawberry Supreme Bars	1 bar	48.5	2.47	9.63	1.11	0.316	0.113	0.053	0.079	1.1	2.45	19.9	81	0.201	71.4	228	32
Orange Raspberry Bars	1 bar	85.9	3.43	18	1.09	0.271	0.097	0.054	0.057	1.32	11.1	50.6	104	0.219	94.9	369	38.8
Peaches and Cream Bars	1 bar	56	2.91	11.5	0.731	0.201	0.109	0.045	0.023	1.32	18.1	3.39	94	0.187	84.1	225	39.7
Piña Colada Bars	1 bar	64.3	1.5	14.8	0.899	0.242	0.069	0.036	0.067	0.551	2	18.9	51.8	0.29	42.3	222	16.7
Peanut Butter Fingers	2½" bar	232	6.69	26.1	3.28	13.1	4.13	5.47	2.77	0	0.74	0.094	17.8	1.26	121	220	121
Granola Fruit Bars	2½" bar	208	3.66	27.4	3.2	10.5	1.15	4.44	4.33	0	20.4	2.5	13.2	1.01	104	171	1.47
Fresh Blueberry Tart	2" wedge	222	1.98	40.2	2.14	6.46	0.82	1.52	3.7	0	5.9	9.2	15.8	1.17	31.8	276	59.9
Bowl Crust Apple Pie	3" wedge	298	2.41	48.7	2.57	11.1	1.49	2.72	6.07	0	3.93	5.11	19.6	1.48	39.4	323	97.2
Mom's Blackberry Pie	2" wedge	246	3.94	57.6	4.95	9.52	1.2	1.9	4.86	0	9.2	13.7	35.8	2.4	60.4	400	122.4
Apple-Berry Crisp	2½" bar	235	2.9	37.25	3.7	9.25	1.2	2.35	5.1	0	6.1	7.25	22.15	1.12	76	254.5	25.8
Variations and Substitutions																	
Almond Milk	1 cup	151	4.77	7.67	2.62	12.5	1.32	7.3	3.31	0	0.058	0.144	107	1.57	134	166	97.4
Cashew Rice Milk	½ cup	158	3.55	19.4	1.13	8.03	1.59	4.7	1.36	0	0	0.053	15.6	1.45	100	113	275
Cashew Rice Cream	½ cup	158	3.55	19.4	1.13	8.03	1.59	4.7	1.36	0	0	0.053	12	1.43	100	113	270
Tofu Whipped Cream	1 tbsp	33.3	0.839	1.65	0.125	2.76	0.36	0.659	1.6	0	0.935	0.077	10.9	0.563	10.1	13.6	11.9
Tofu Sour Cream	1 tbsp	35.3	1	0.733	0.152	3.32	0.432	0.791	1.92	0	1.14	0.368	13.1	0.668	12.1	16.3	54.2
Fruit Cream	¼ cup	39.6	0.75	7.41	0.476	0.902	0.173	0.454	0.197	0	0.423	0.372	5.1	0.371	24.6	68.1	166
Tofu Mayonnaise	1 tbsp	20.8	1.01	1.19	0.153	1.49	0.208	0.794	0.411	0	1.14	0.49	13.2	0.674	12.1	16.8	54.2
Tofu Tartar Sauce	1 tbsp	17.2	0.54	1.81	0.137	0.99	0.133	0.231	0.571	0	0.744	0.936	7.41	0.355	7.04	16.1	51.4
Sweet and Sour Sauce	1 tbsp	8.68	0.14	0.02	0.04	0.015	0.002	0	0.004	0	0.143	1.73	1.75	0.075	3.11	21.1	94.25
Vinegarless Ketchup	1 tbsp	10.6	0.341	2.47	0.525	0.084	0.013	0.012	0.036	0	142	8.42	4.16	0.199	8.33	82.8	6.64
Chili Powder Substitute	1 tbsp	11.8	0.539	2.45	0.589	0.303	0.034	0.018	0.116	0	83	2.98	32.1	1.07	15	84.3	2.54
Chickenlike Seasoning	1 tbsp	5.75	0.72	0.83	0.32	0.033	0.011	0.016	0.003	0	1.1	0.128	5.3	0.343	31.7	36.6	68.9
Parmesan Cheese, Nondairy	1 tbsp	39.7	2.51	3.14	1.79	2.28	0.335	0.866	0.984	0	0.198	0.474	53.8	1.4	104	107	14.1
Pimento Cheese, Nondairy	2 tbsp	35	1.52	4.55	1.08	1.39	0.243	0.691	0.334	0	15	3.08	8.03	0.58	33.4	59.6	109

INDEX OF RECIPES

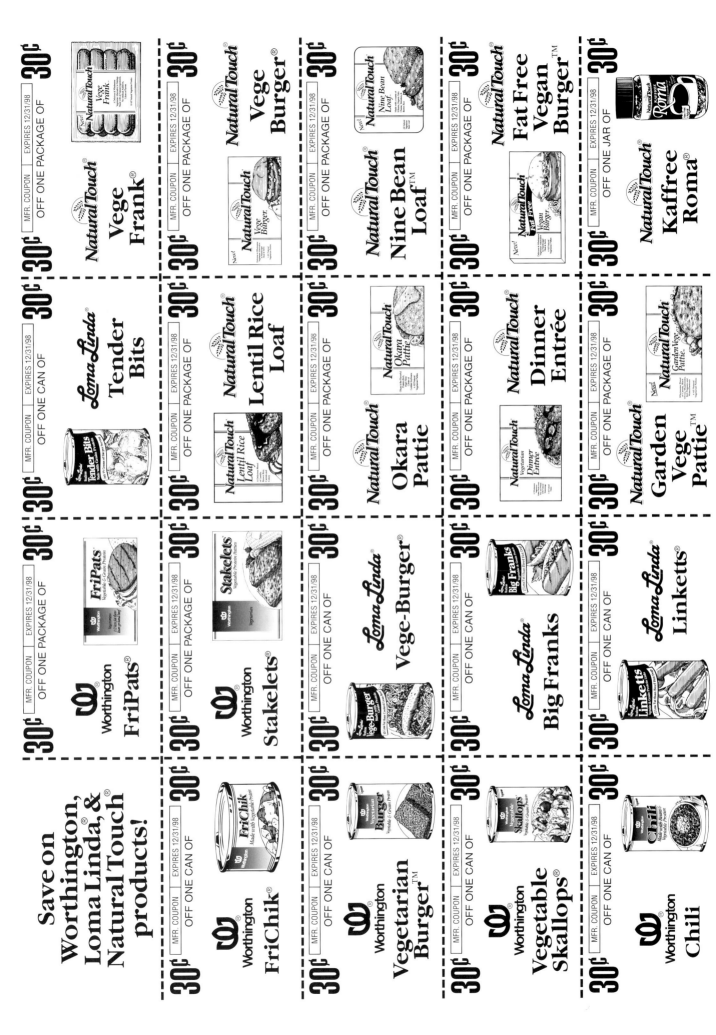

Save on Worthington, Loma Linda, & Natural Touch products!

Each coupon below reads:

30¢ — MFR. COUPON — EXPIRES 12/31/98

RETAILER: Worthington Foods will reimburse you for the face value of this coupon plus 8¢ handling, provided you and the consumer have complied with the terms of the offer. Void if copied, transferred, prohibited, taxed or restricted. Customer must pay any sales tax. Any other use constitutes fraud. Cash value 1/100¢. For redemption, mail to Worthington Foods, Inc., LMS Dept. 2690, P.O. Box 909, Tecate, CA 91980-0909. **LIMIT ONE COUPON PER PURCHASE.**

Coupons:

- Save 30¢ on one package of Natural Touch Vege Frank®
- Save 30¢ on one can of Loma Linda Tender Bits
- Save 30¢ on one package of Natural Touch Vege Burger®
- Save 30¢ on one package of Worthington FriPats®
- Save 30¢ on one package of Natural Touch Nine Bean Loaf™
- Save 30¢ on one package of Natural Touch Lentil Rice Loaf
- Save 30¢ on one can of Worthington Stakelets®
- Save 30¢ on one can of Worthington FriChik®
- Save 30¢ on one package of Natural Touch Fat Free Vegan Burger™
- Save 30¢ on one package of Natural Touch Okara Pattie
- Save 30¢ on one can of Loma Linda Vege-Burger®
- Save 30¢ on one can of Worthington Vegetarian Burger™
- Save 30¢ on one jar of Natural Touch Kaffree Roma®
- Save 30¢ on one package of Natural Touch Dinner Entrée
- Save 30¢ on one can of Loma Linda Big Franks
- Save 30¢ on one can of Worthington Vegetable Skallops®
- Save 30¢ on one package of Natural Touch Garden Vege Pattie™
- Save 30¢ on one can of Loma Linda Linketts®
- Save 30¢ on one can of Worthington Chili